W9-BVZ-539

SOUR PICKLES

CLIO ISADORA

AVERY HILL PUBLISHING

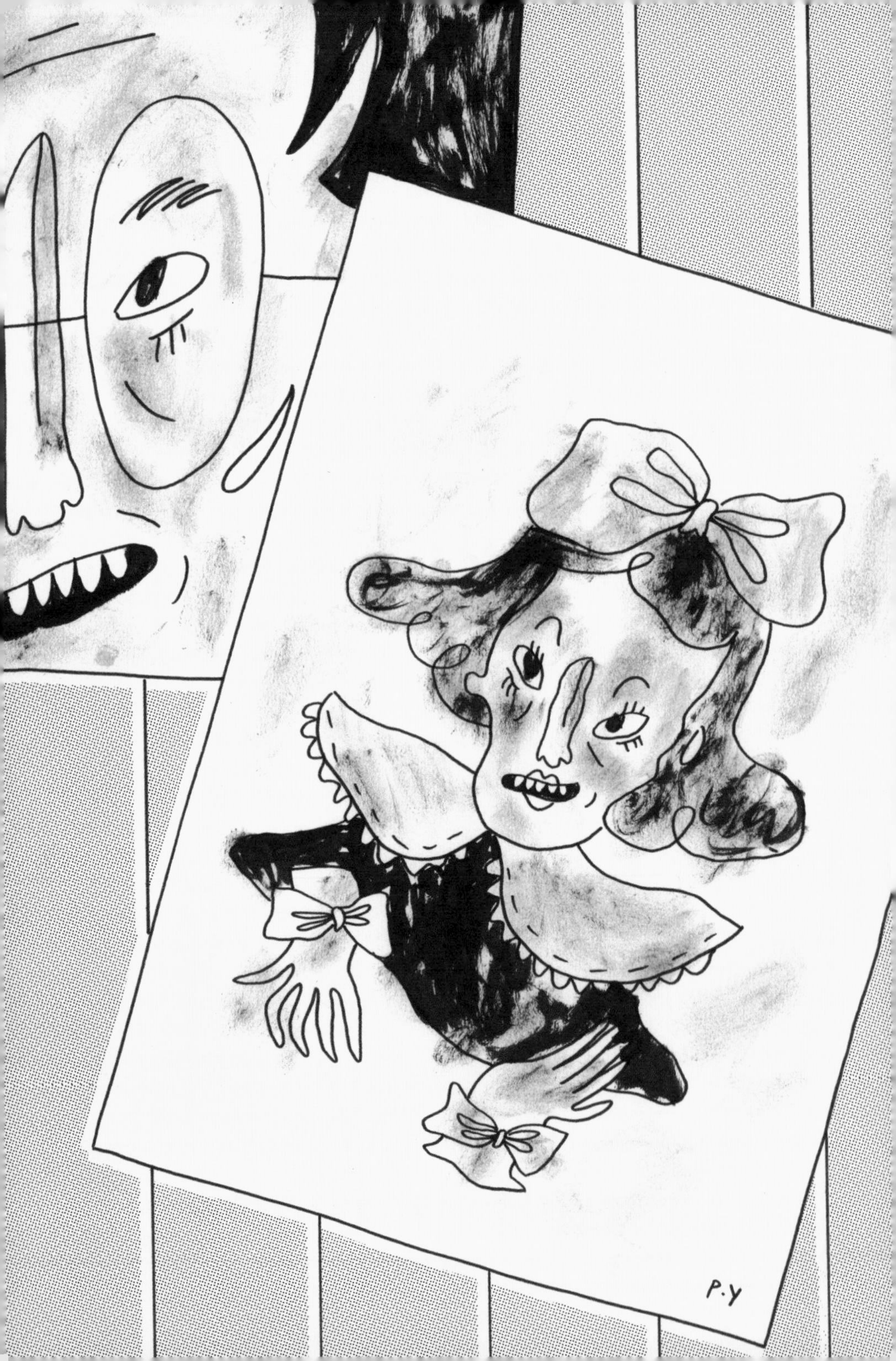
P.Y

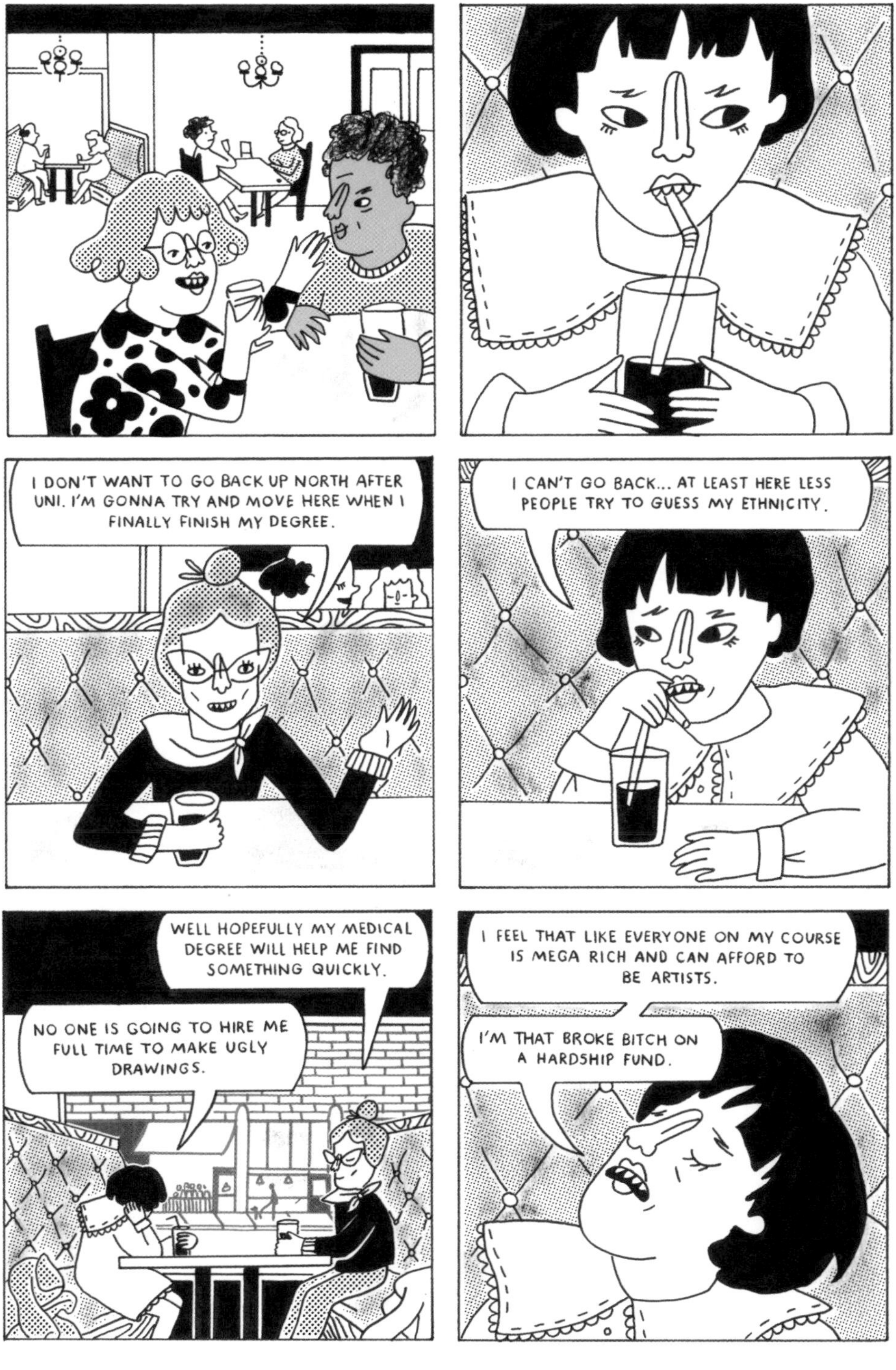
I DON'T WANT TO GO BACK UP NORTH AFTER UNI. I'M GONNA TRY AND MOVE HERE WHEN I FINALLY FINISH MY DEGREE.
I CAN'T GO BACK... AT LEAST HERE LESS PEOPLE TRY TO GUESS MY ETHNICITY.
WELL HOPEFULLY MY MEDICAL DEGREE WILL HELP ME FIND SOMETHING QUICKLY.
NO ONE IS GOING TO HIRE ME FULL TIME TO MAKE UGLY DRAWINGS.
I FEEL THAT LIKE EVERYONE ON MY COURSE IS MEGA RICH AND CAN AFFORD TO BE ARTISTS.
I'M THAT BROKE BITCH ON A HARDSHIP FUND.

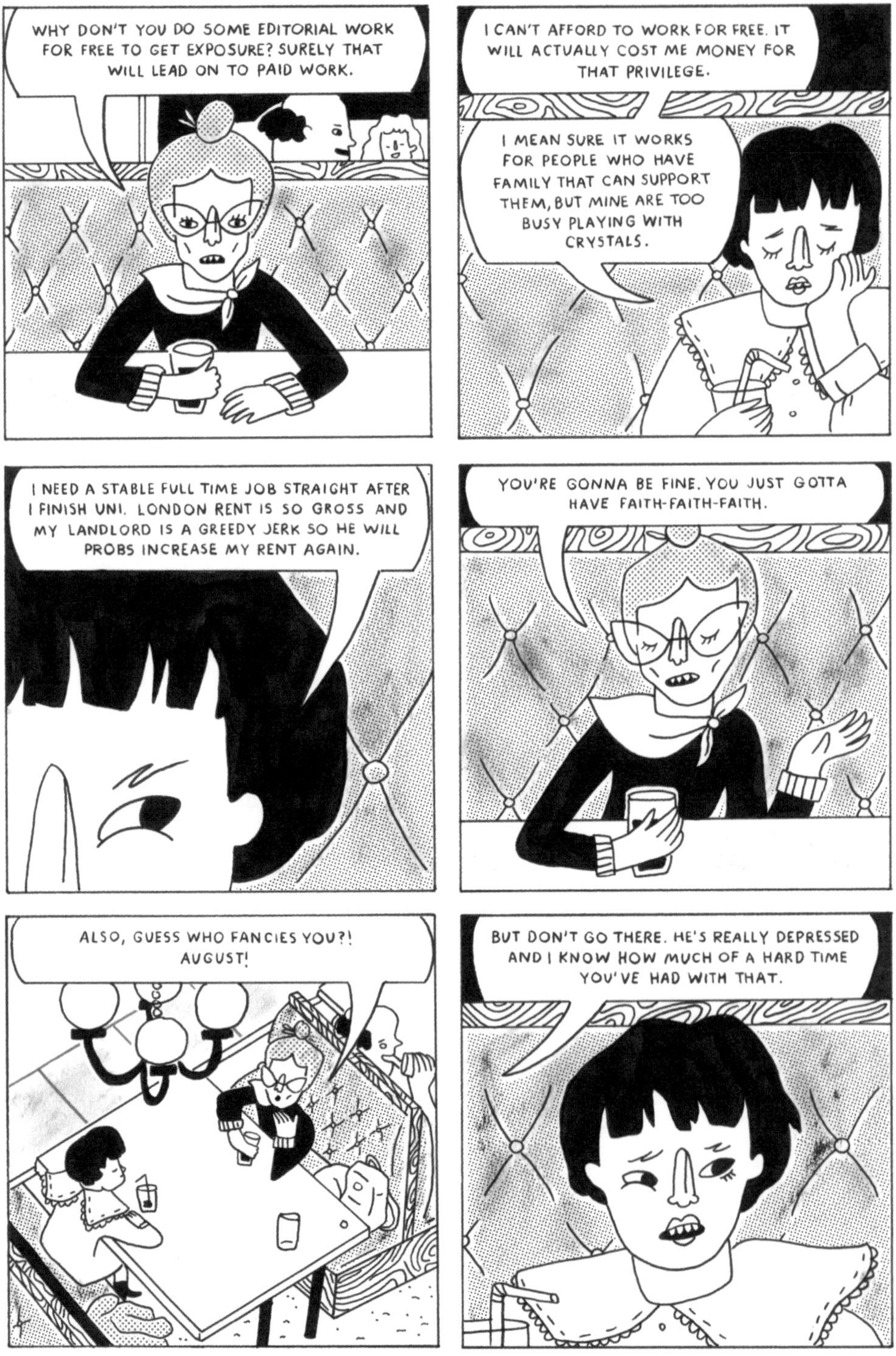
WHY DON'T YOU DO SOME EDITORIAL WORK FOR FREE TO GET EXPOSURE? SURELY THAT WILL LEAD ON TO PAID WORK.
I CAN'T AFFORD TO WORK FOR FREE. IT WILL ACTUALLY COST ME MONEY FOR THAT PRIVILEGE.
I MEAN SURE IT WORKS FOR PEOPLE WHO HAVE FAMILY THAT CAN SUPPORT THEM, BUT MINE ARE TOO BUSY PLAYING WITH CRYSTALS.
I NEED A STABLE FULL TIME JOB STRAIGHT AFTER I FINISH UNI. LONDON RENT IS SO GROSS AND MY LANDLORD IS A GREEDY JERK SO HE WILL PROBS INCREASE MY RENT AGAIN.
YOU'RE GONNA BE FINE. YOU JUST GOTTA HAVE FAITH-FAITH-FAITH.
ALSO, GUESS WHO FANCIES YOU?! AUGUST!
BUT DON'T GO THERE. HE'S REALLY DEPRESSED AND I KNOW HOW MUCH OF A HARD TIME YOU'VE HAD WITH THAT.

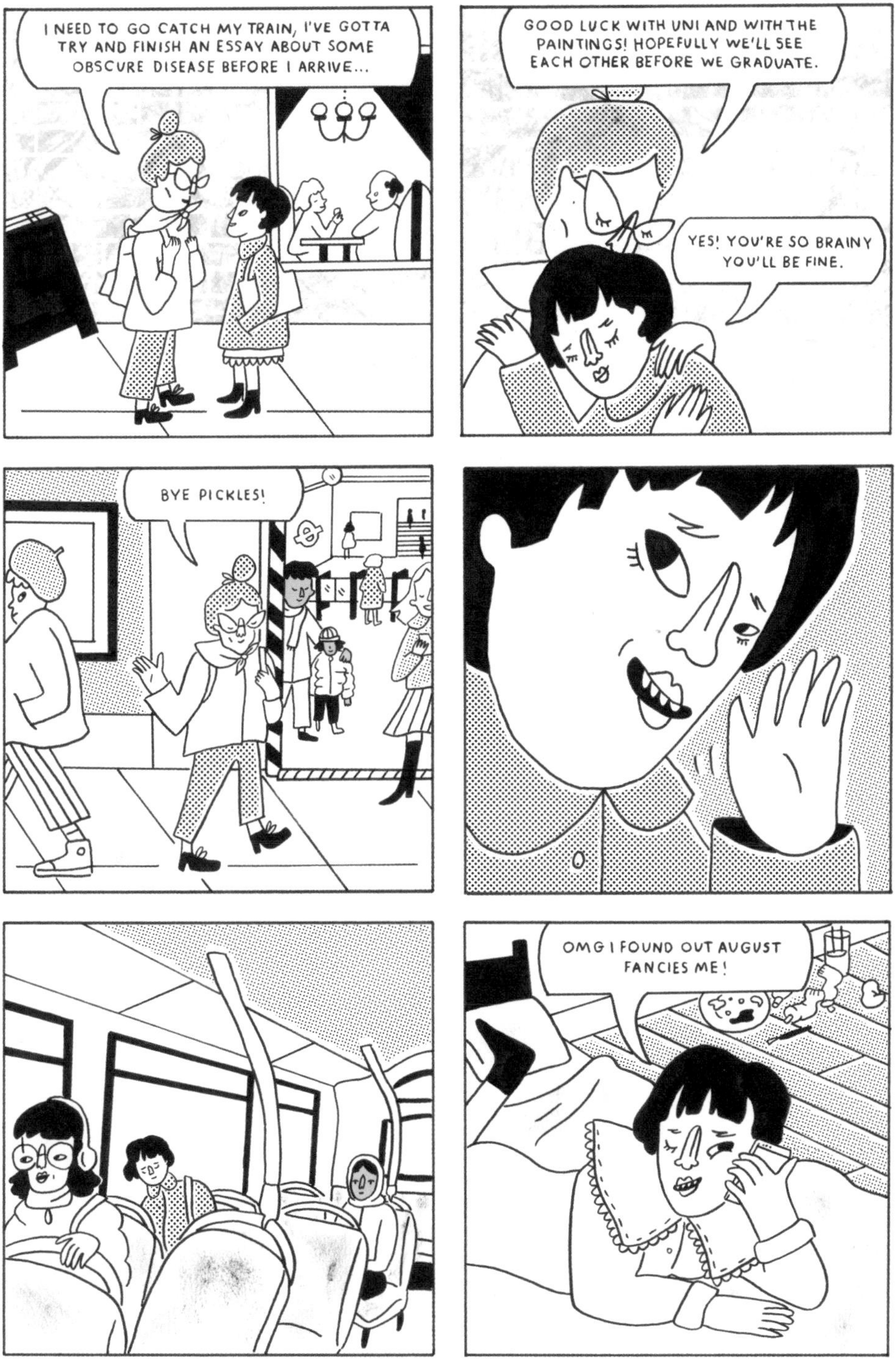
I NEED TO GO CATCH MY TRAIN, I'VE GOTTA TRY AND FINISH AN ESSAY ABOUT SOME OBSCURE DISEASE BEFORE I ARRIVE...
GOOD LUCK WITH UNI AND WITH THE PAINTINGS! HOPEFULLY WE'LL SEE EACH OTHER BEFORE WE GRADUATE.
YES! YOU'RE SO BRAINY YOU'LL BE FINE.
BYE PICKLES!
OMG I FOUND OUT AUGUST FANCIES ME!

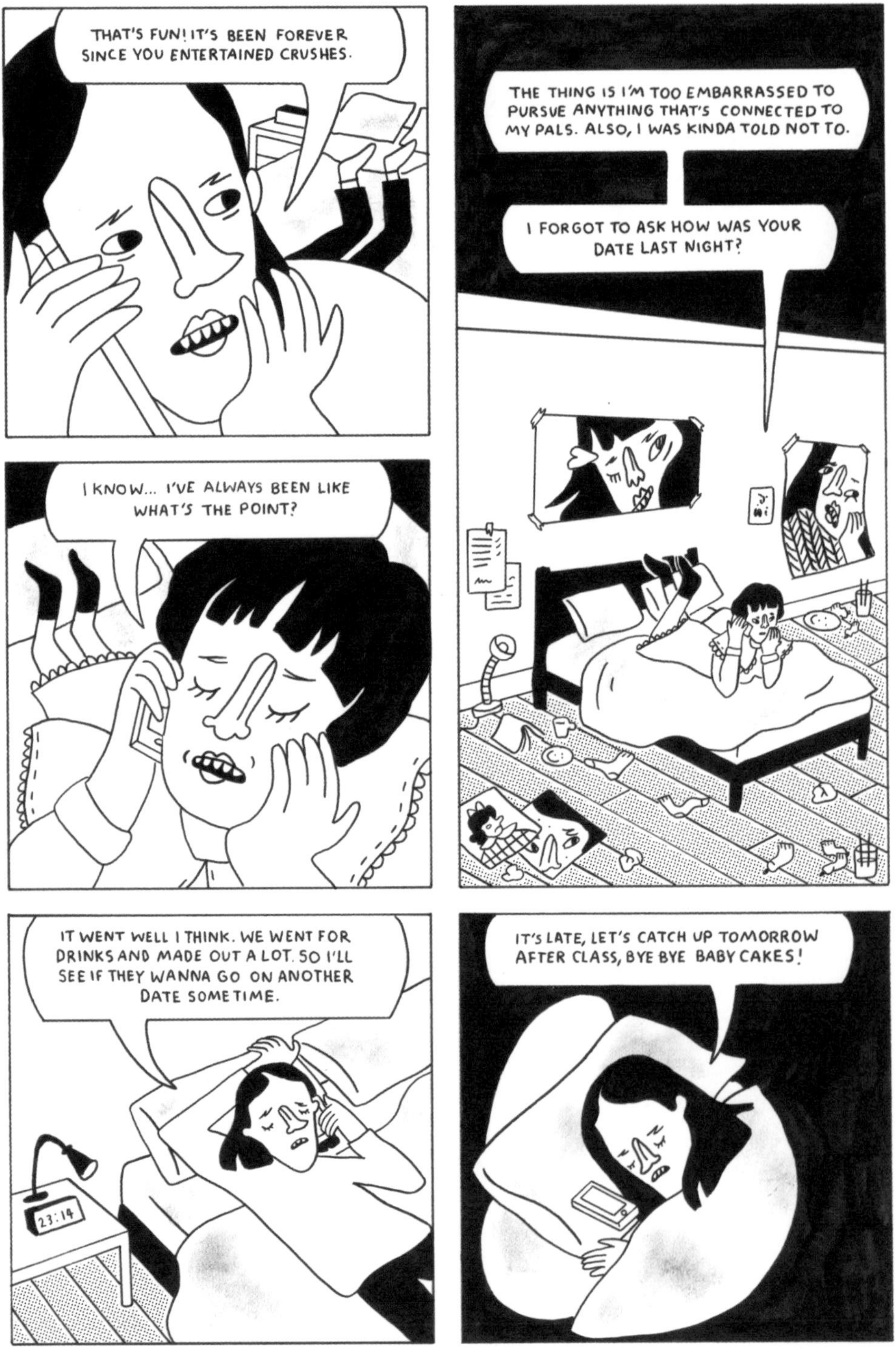
THAT'S FUN! IT'S BEEN FOREVER SINCE YOU ENTERTAINED CRUSHES.
I KNOW... I'VE ALWAYS BEEN LIKE WHAT'S THE POINT?
THE THING IS I'M TOO EMBARRASSED TO PURSUE ANYTHING THAT'S CONNECTED TO MY PALS. ALSO, I WAS KINDA TOLD NOT TO.
I FORGOT TO ASK HOW WAS YOUR DATE LAST NIGHT?
IT WENT WELL I THINK. WE WENT FOR DRINKS AND MADE OUT A LOT. SO I'LL SEE IF THEY WANNA GO ON ANOTHER DATE SOMETIME.
23:14
IT'S LATE, LET'S CATCH UP TOMORROW AFTER CLASS, BYE BYE BABY CAKES!

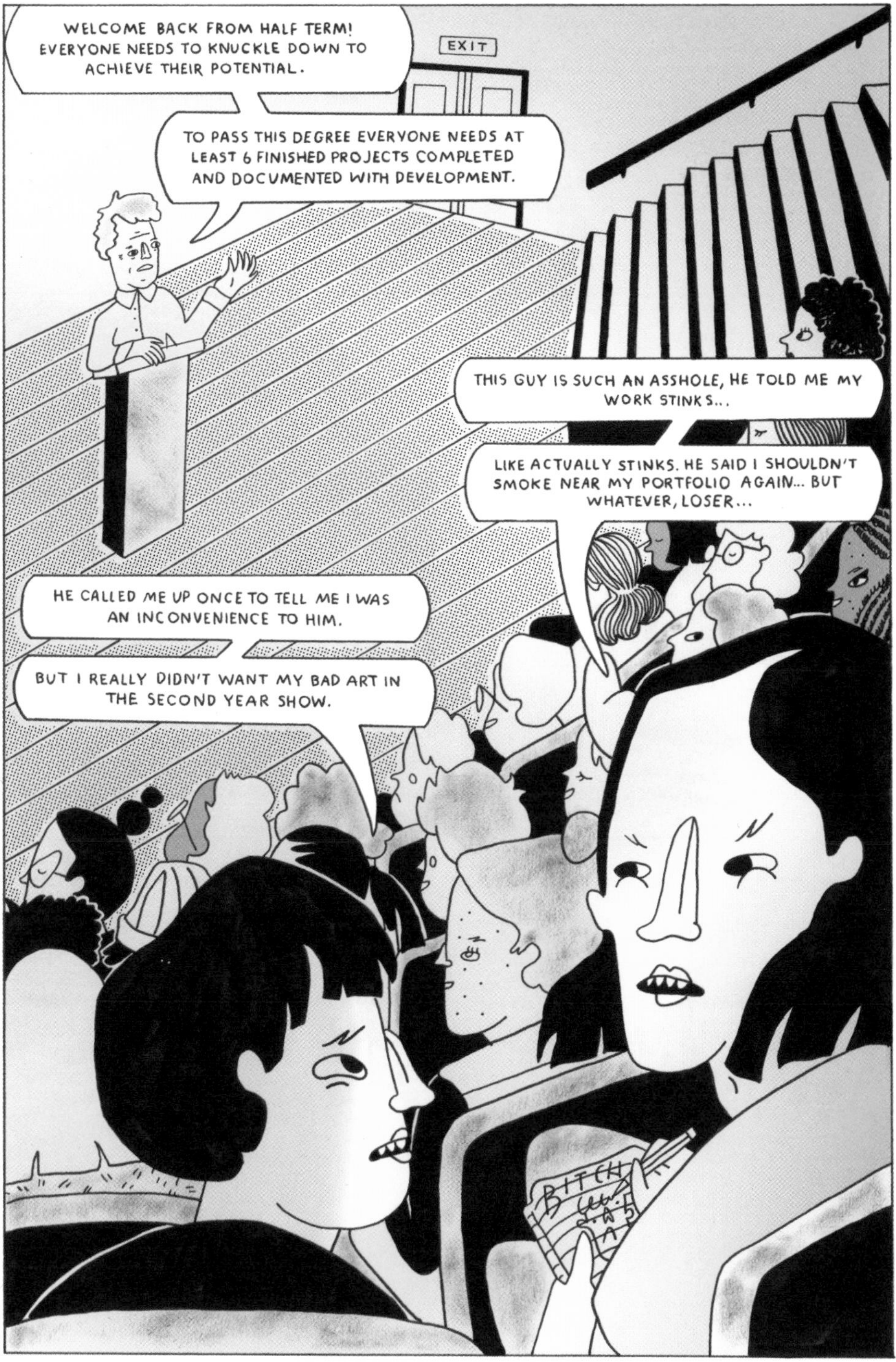
EXIT
WELCOME BACK FROM HALF TERM! EVERYONE NEEDS TO KNUCKLE DOWN TO ACHIEVE THEIR POTENTIAL.
TO PASS THIS DEGREE EVERYONE NEEDS AT LEAST 6 FINISHED PROJECTS COMPLETED AND DOCUMENTED WITH DEVELOPMENT.
THIS GUY IS SUCH AN ASSHOLE, HE TOLD ME MY WORK STINKS...
LIKE ACTUALLY STINKS. HE SAID I SHOULDN'T SMOKE NEAR MY PORTFOLIO AGAIN... BUT WHATEVER, LOSER...
HE CALLED ME UP ONCE TO TELL ME I WAS AN INCONVENIENCE TO HIM.
BUT I REALLY DIDN'T WANT MY BAD ART IN THE SECOND YEAR SHOW.
BITCH

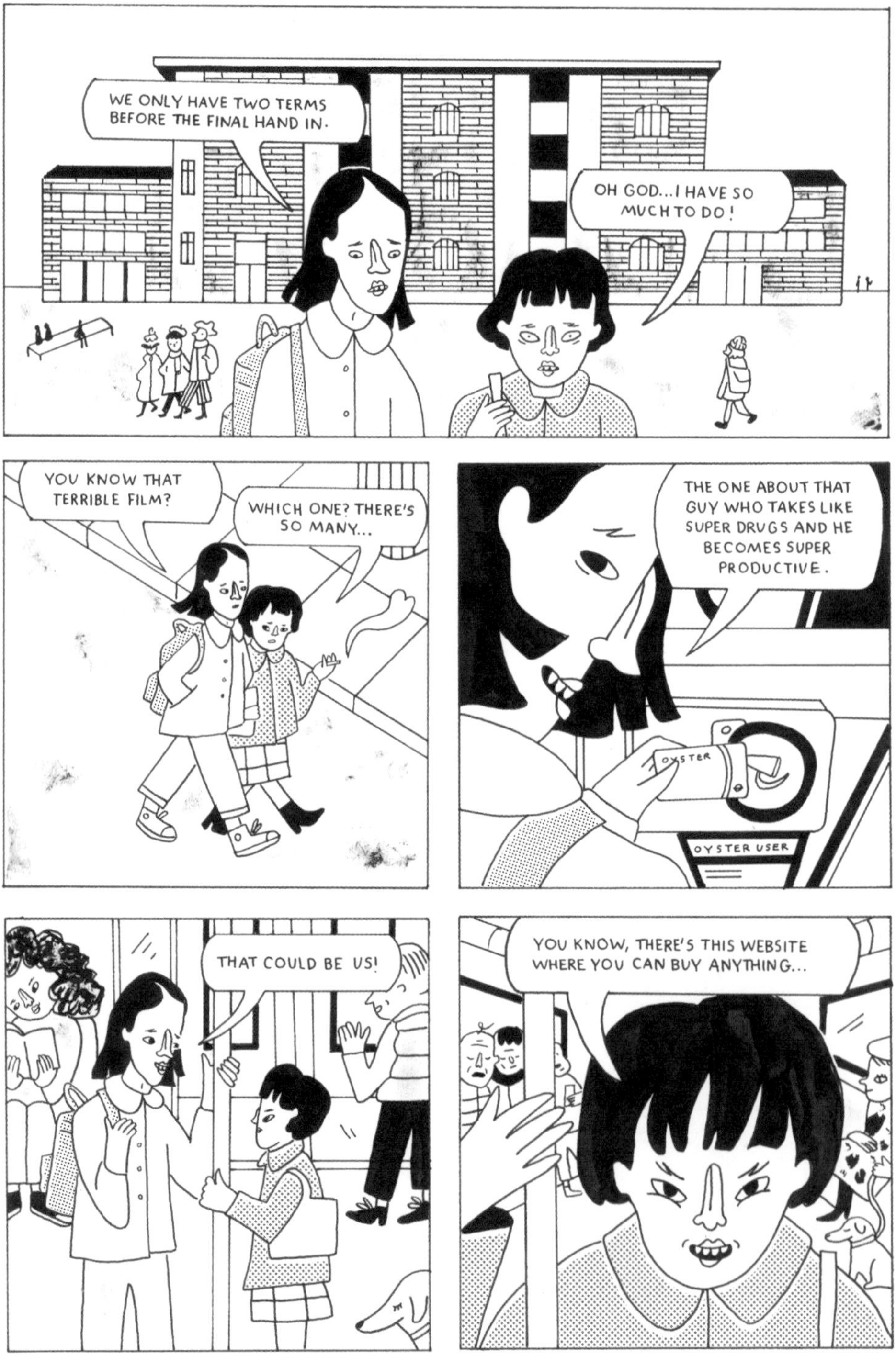
WE ONLY HAVE TWO TERMS BEFORE THE FINAL HAND IN.
OH GOD... I HAVE SO MUCH TO DO!
YOU KNOW THAT TERRIBLE FILM?
WHICH ONE? THERE'S SO MANY...
THE ONE ABOUT THAT GUY WHO TAKES LIKE SUPER DRUGS AND HE BECOMES SUPER PRODUCTIVE.
OYSTER
OYSTER USER
THAT COULD BE US!
YOU KNOW, THERE'S THIS WEBSITE WHERE YOU CAN BUY ANYTHING...

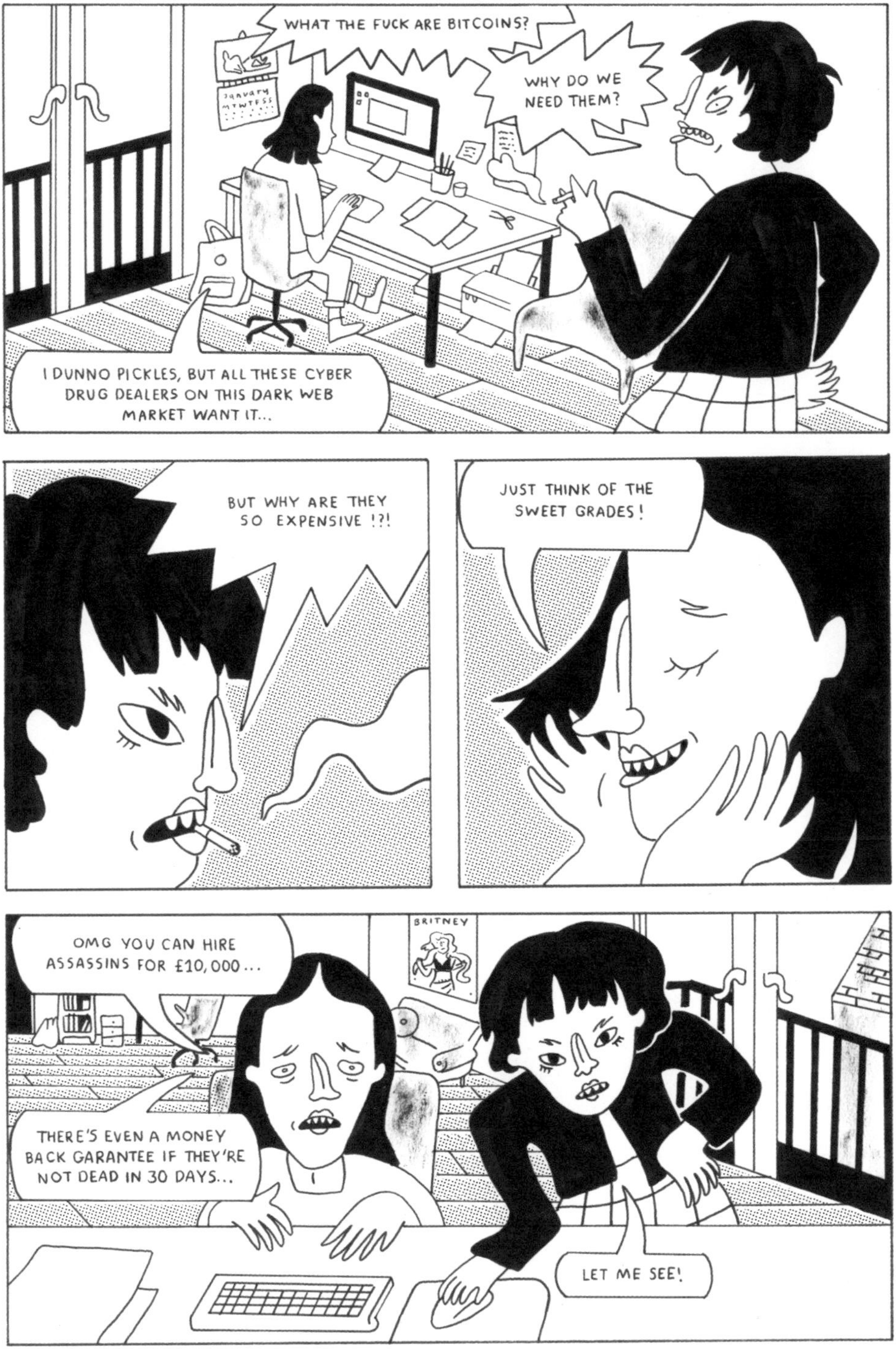
WHAT THE FUCK ARE BITCOINS?
WHY DO WE NEED THEM?
I DUNNO PICKLES, BUT ALL THESE CYBER DRUG DEALERS ON THIS DARK WEB MARKET WANT IT...
BUT WHY ARE THEY SO EXPENSIVE !?!
JUST THINK OF THE SWEET GRADES!
OMG YOU CAN HIRE ASSASSINS FOR £10,000...
THERE'S EVEN A MONEY BACK GARANTEE IF THEY'RE NOT DEAD IN 30 DAYS...
LET ME SEE!
BRITNEY
January
MTWTFSS

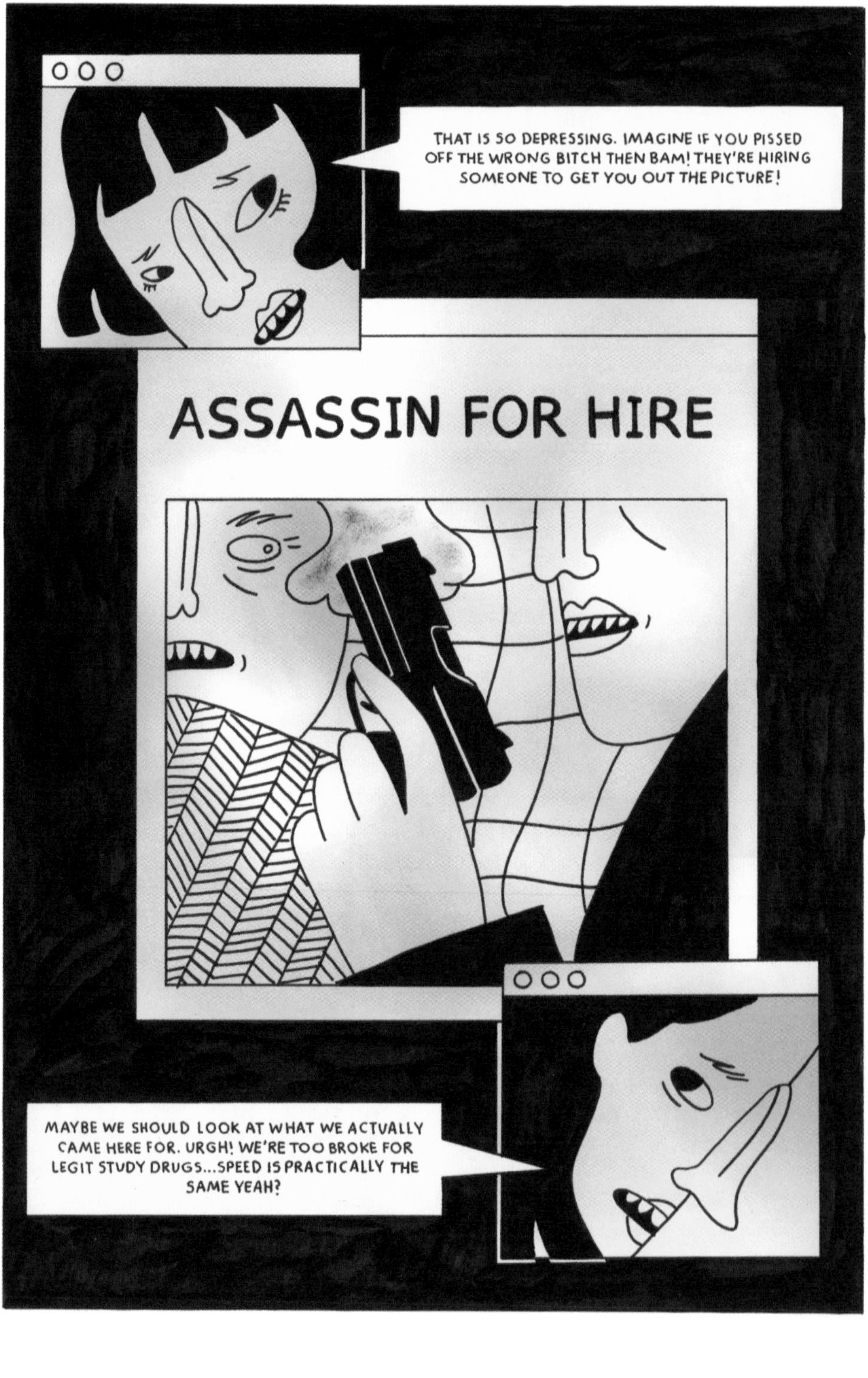
THAT IS SO DEPRESSING. IMAGINE IF YOU PISSED OFF THE WRONG BITCH THEN BAM! THEY'RE HIRING SOMEONE TO GET YOU OUT THE PICTURE!
ASSASSIN FOR HIRE
MAYBE WE SHOULD LOOK AT WHAT WE ACTUALLY CAME HERE FOR. URGH! WE'RE TOO BROKE FOR LEGIT STUDY DRUGS...SPEED IS PRACTICALLY THE SAME YEAH?

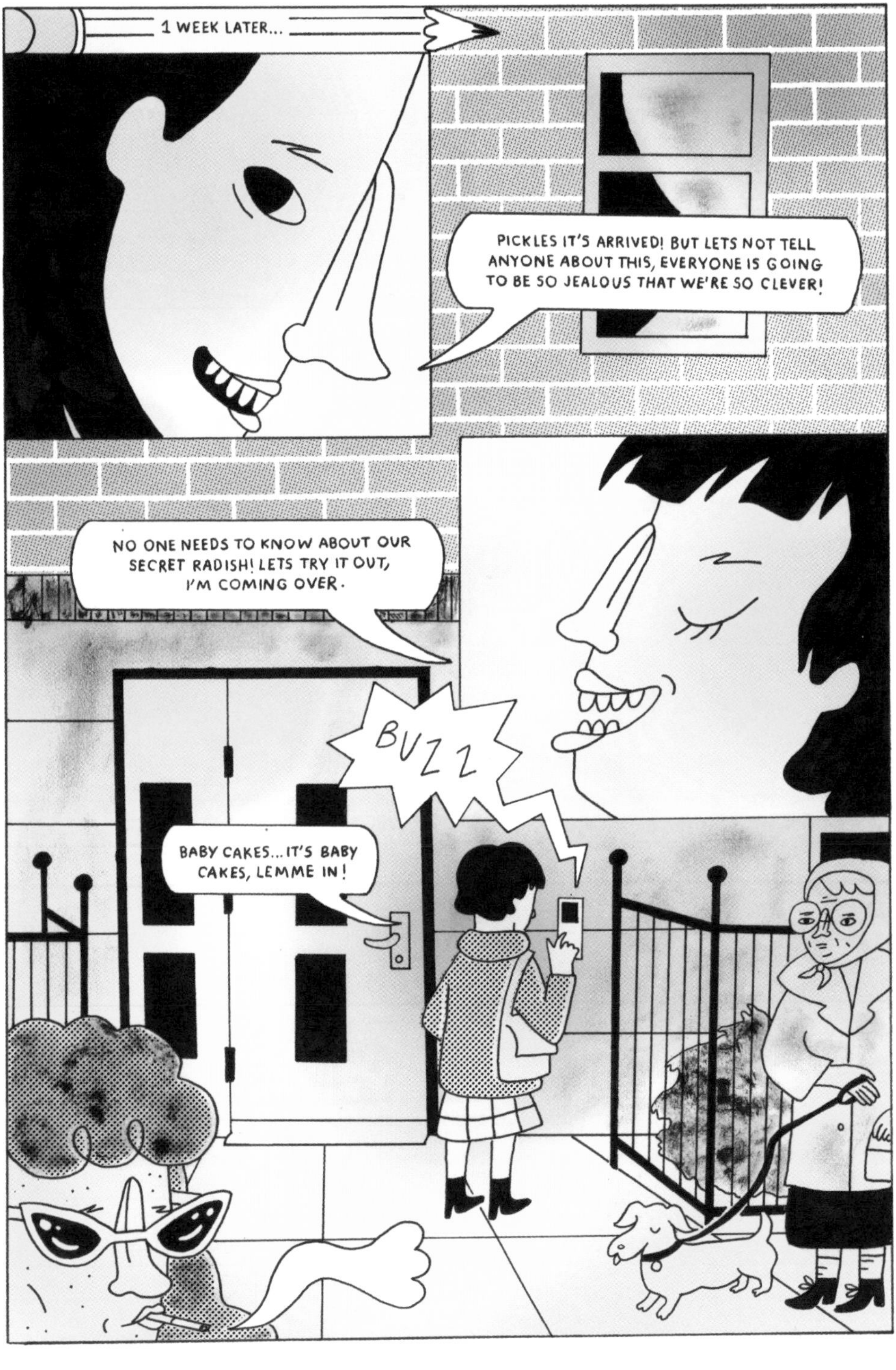
1 WEEK LATER...
PICKLES IT'S ARRIVED! BUT LETS NOT TELL ANYONE ABOUT THIS, EVERYONE IS GOING TO BE SO JEALOUS THAT WE'RE SO CLEVER!
NO ONE NEEDS TO KNOW ABOUT OUR SECRET RADISH! LETS TRY IT OUT, I'M COMING OVER.
BUZZ
BABY CAKES... IT'S BABY CAKES, LEMME IN!

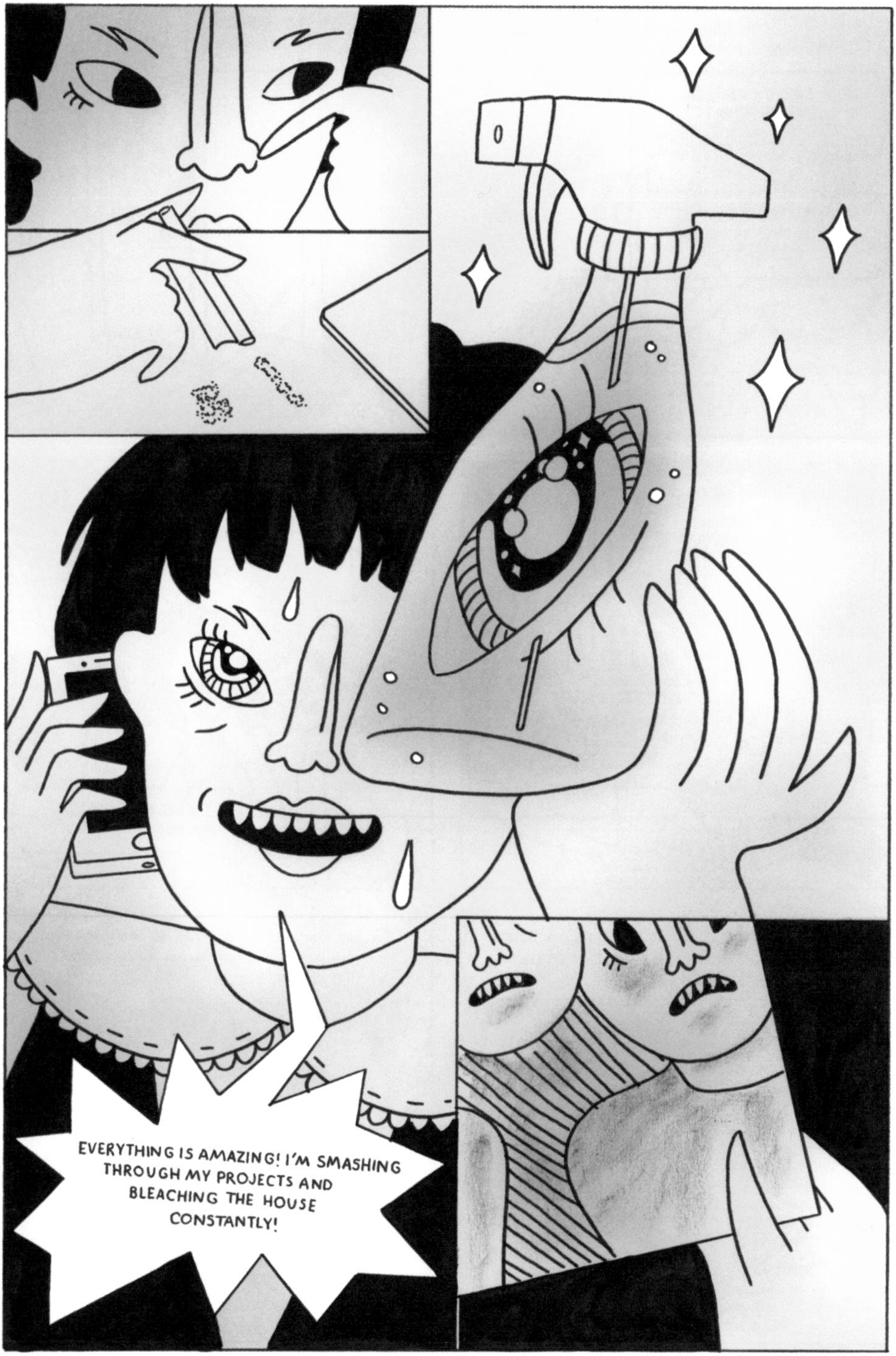
EVERYTHING IS AMAZING! I'M SMASHING THROUGH MY PROJECTS AND BLEACHING THE HOUSE CONSTANTLY!

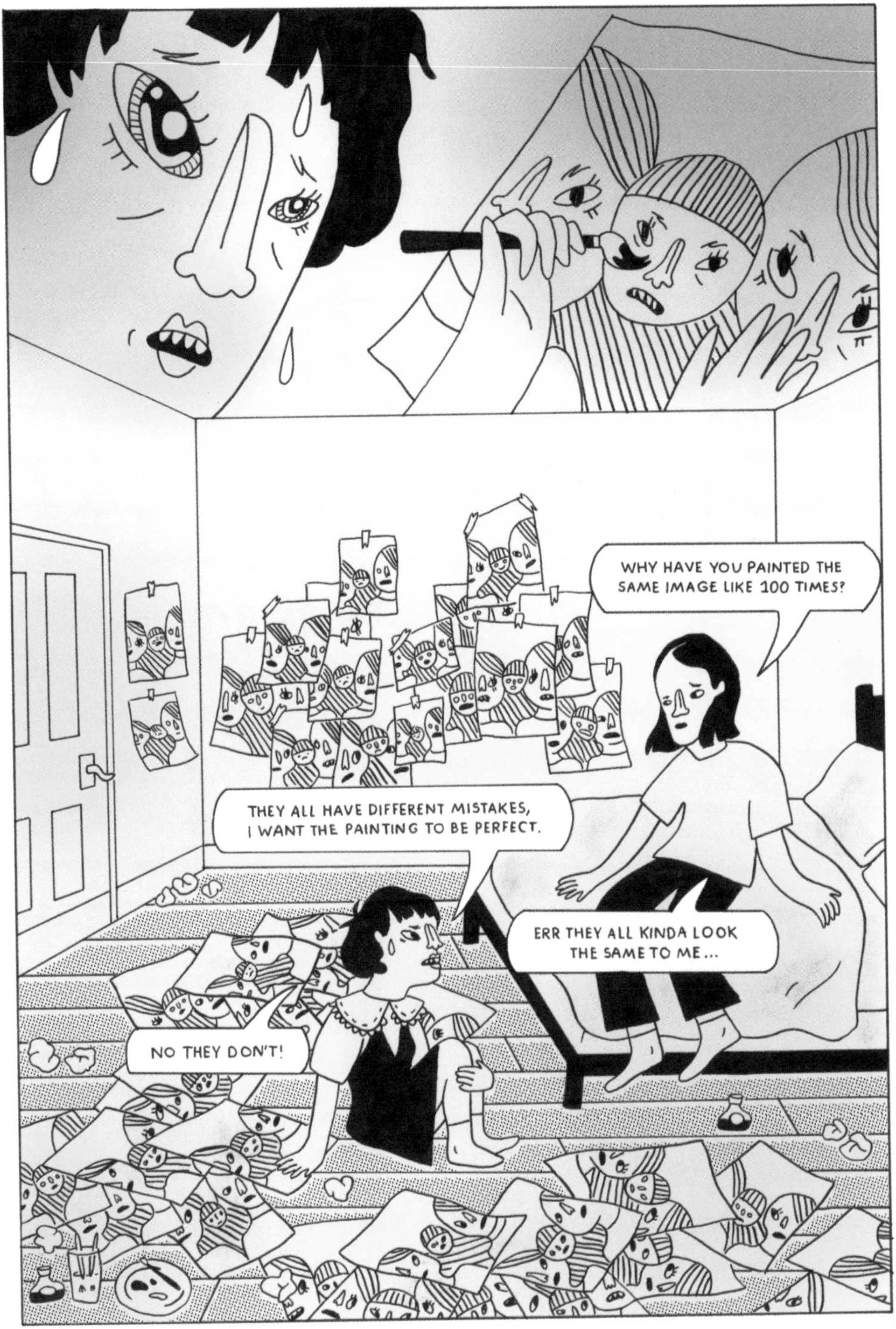
WHY HAVE YOU PAINTED THE SAME IMAGE LIKE 100 TIMES?
THEY ALL HAVE DIFFERENT MISTAKES, I WANT THE PAINTING TO BE PERFECT.
ERR THEY ALL KINDA LOOK THE SAME TO ME...
NO THEY DON'T!

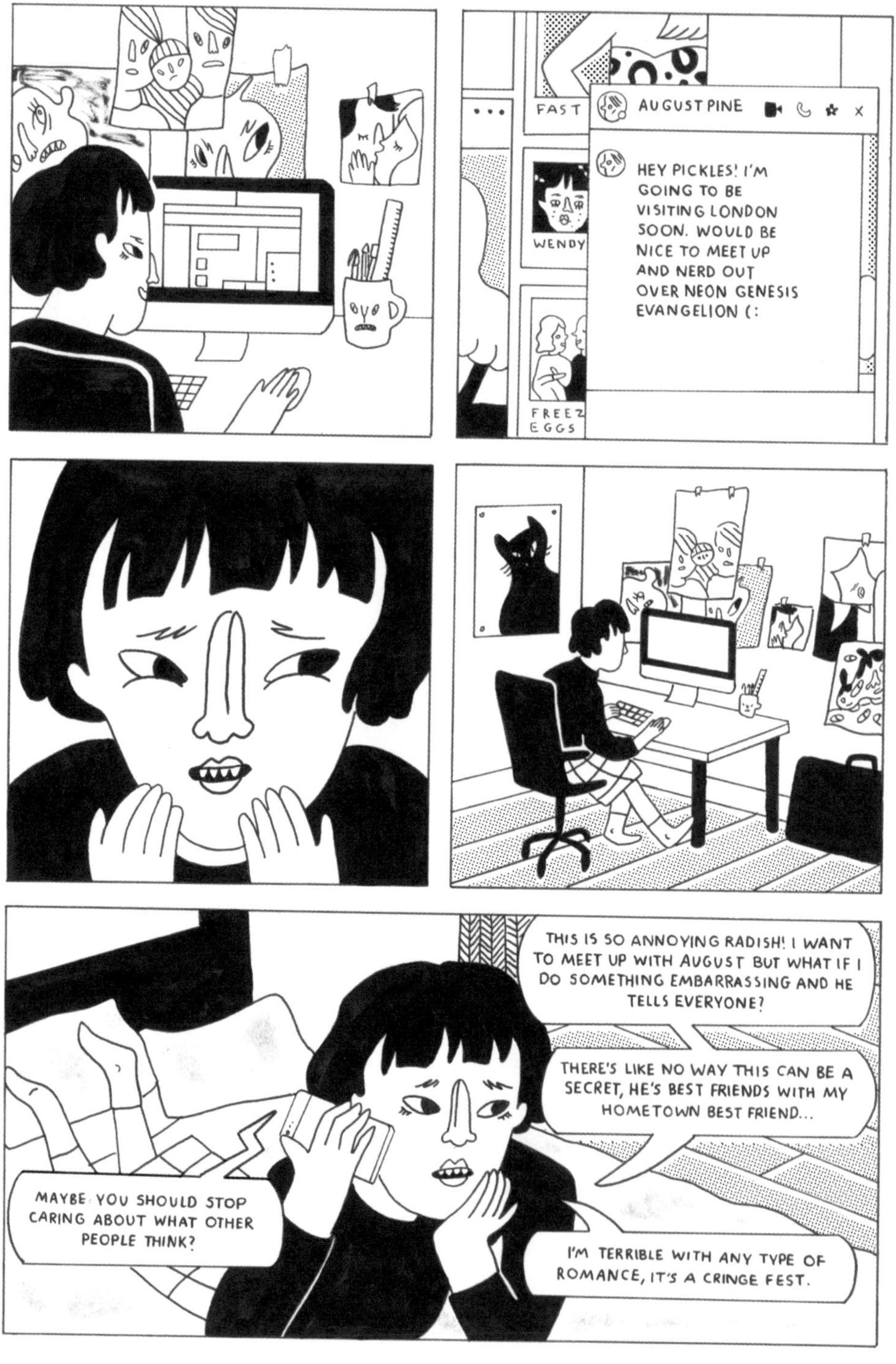
FAST
WENDY
FREEZ
EGGS
AUGUSTPINE
HEY PICKLES! I'M GOING TO BE VISITING LONDON SOON. WOULD BE NICE TO MEET UP AND NERD OUT OVER NEON GENESIS EVANGELION (:
THIS IS SO ANNOYING RADISH! I WANT TO MEET UP WITH AUGUST BUT WHAT IF I DO SOMETHING EMBARRASSING AND HE TELLS EVERYONE?
THERE'S LIKE NO WAY THIS CAN BE A SECRET, HE'S BEST FRIENDS WITH MY HOMETOWN BEST FRIEND...
MAYBE YOU SHOULD STOP CARING ABOUT WHAT OTHER PEOPLE THINK?
I'M TERRIBLE WITH ANY TYPE OF ROMANCE, IT'S A CRINGE FEST.

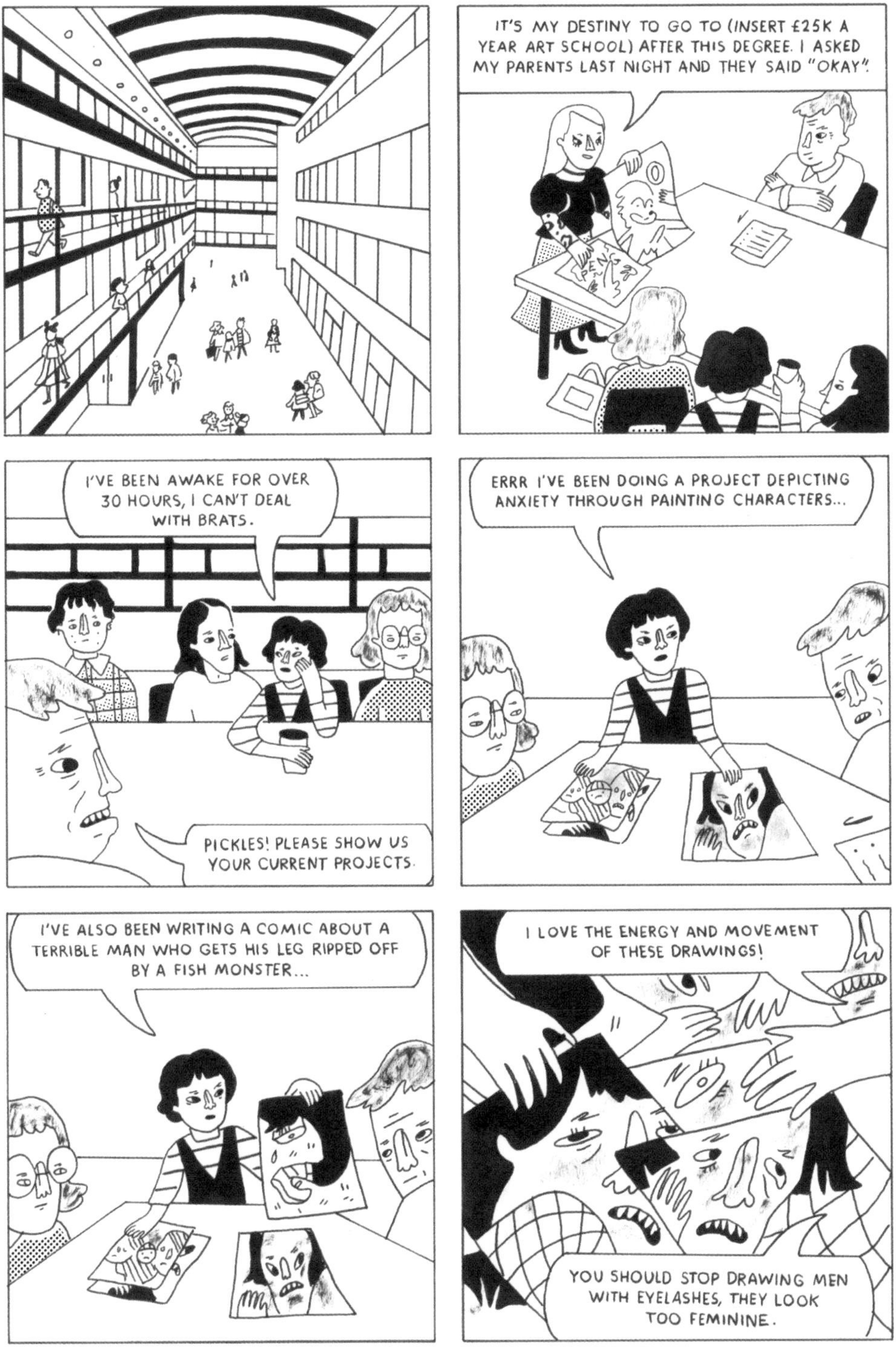
IT'S MY DESTINY TO GO TO (INSERT £25K A YEAR ART SCHOOL) AFTER THIS DEGREE. I ASKED MY PARENTS LAST NIGHT AND THEY SAID "OKAY".
I'VE BEEN AWAKE FOR OVER 30 HOURS, I CAN'T DEAL WITH BRATS.
PICKLES! PLEASE SHOW US YOUR CURRENT PROJECTS.
ERRR I'VE BEEN DOING A PROJECT DEPICTING ANXIETY THROUGH PAINTING CHARACTERS...
I'VE ALSO BEEN WRITING A COMIC ABOUT A TERRIBLE MAN WHO GETS HIS LEG RIPPED OFF BY A FISH MONSTER...
I LOVE THE ENERGY AND MOVEMENT OF THESE DRAWINGS!
YOU SHOULD STOP DRAWING MEN WITH EYELASHES, THEY LOOK TOO FEMININE.

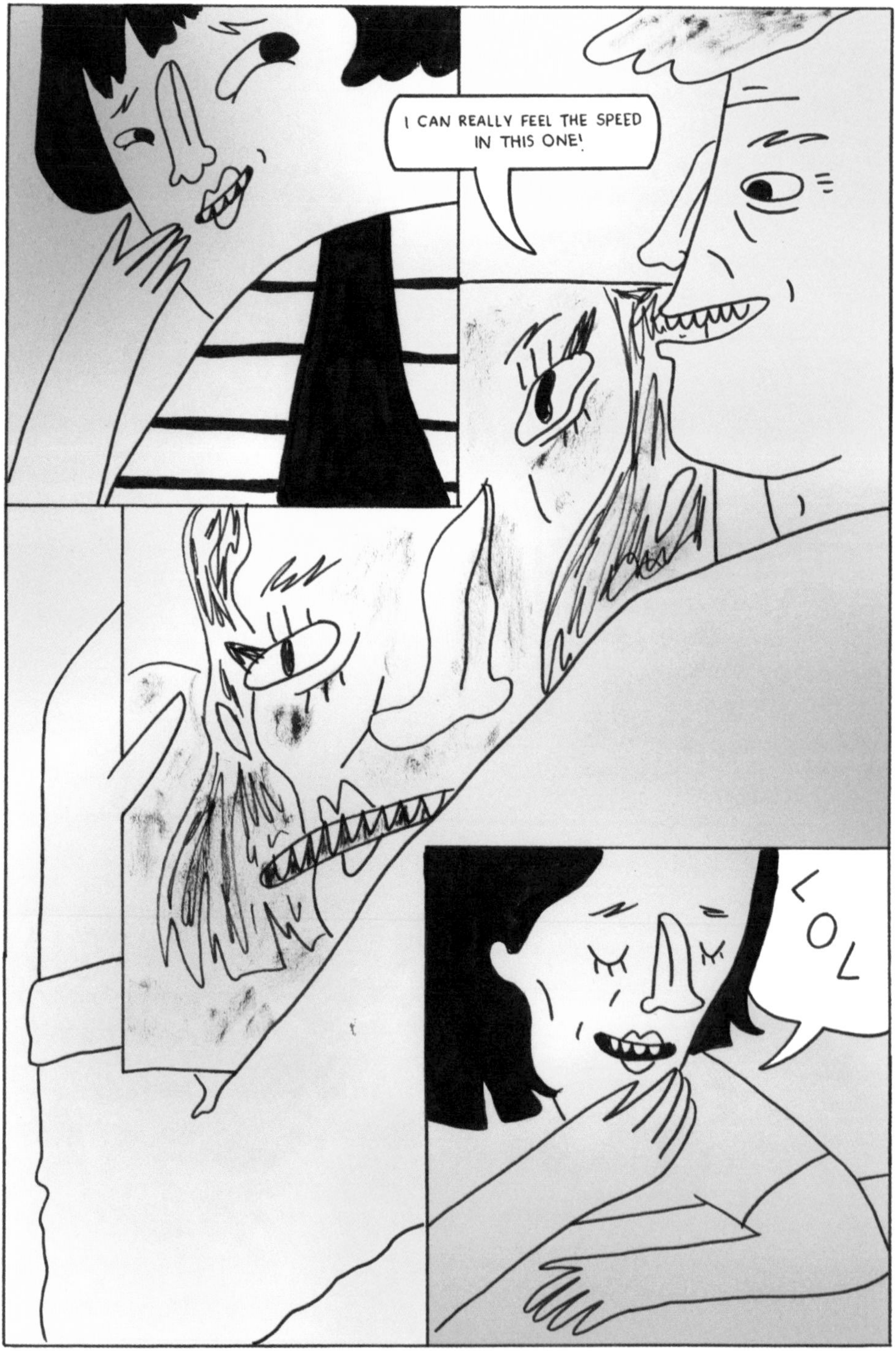
I CAN REALLY FEEL THE SPEED IN THIS ONE!
LOL

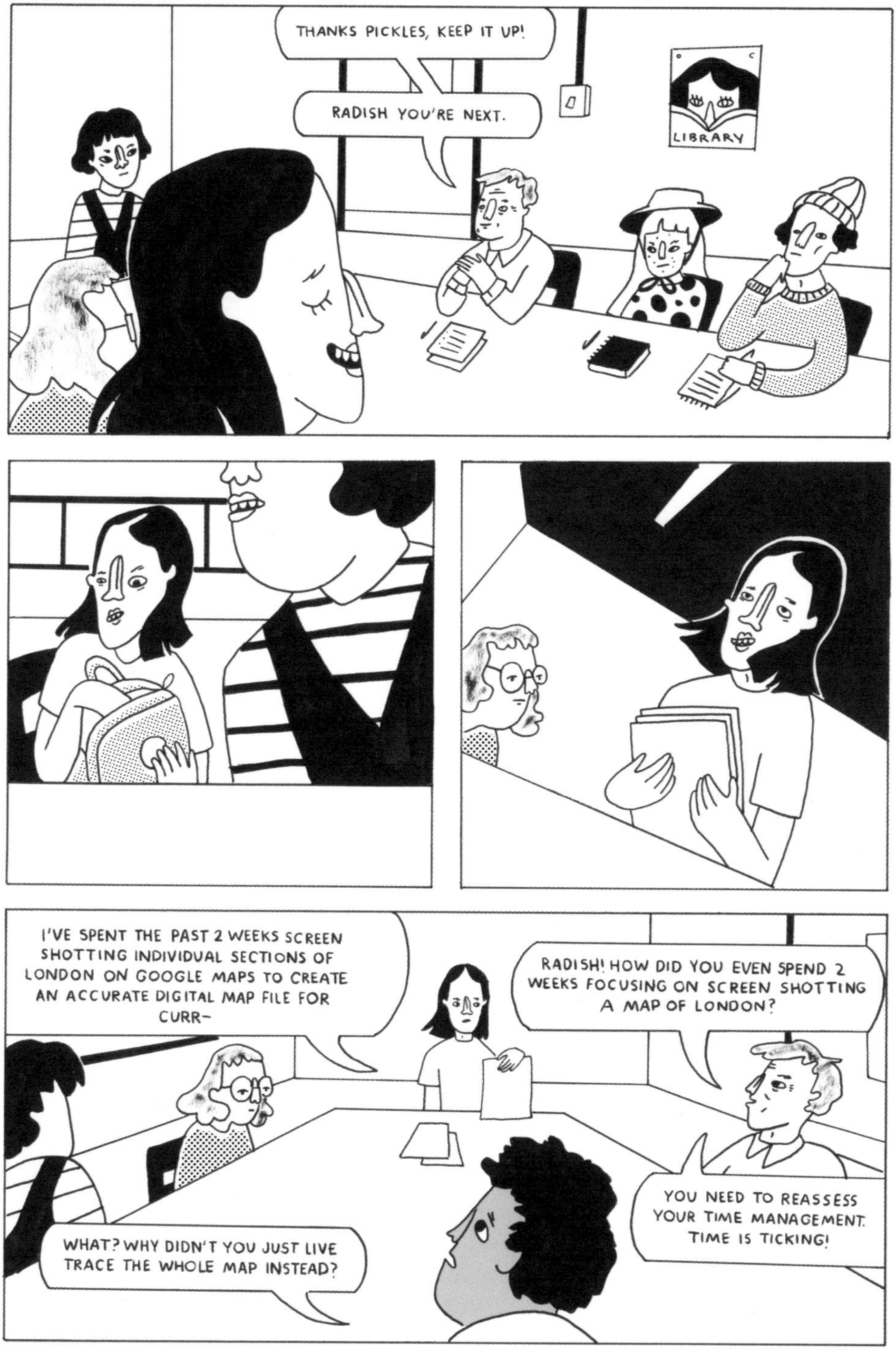
THANKS PICKLES, KEEP IT UP!
RADISH YOU'RE NEXT.
LIBRARY
I'VE SPENT THE PAST 2 WEEKS SCREEN SHOTTING INDIVIDUAL SECTIONS OF LONDON ON GOOGLE MAPS TO CREATE AN ACCURATE DIGITAL MAP FILE FOR CURR–
RADISH! HOW DID YOU EVEN SPEND 2 WEEKS FOCUSING ON SCREEN SHOTTING A MAP OF LONDON?
YOU NEED TO REASSESS YOUR TIME MANAGEMENT. TIME IS TICKING!
WHAT? WHY DIDN'T YOU JUST LIVE TRACE THE WHOLE MAP INSTEAD?

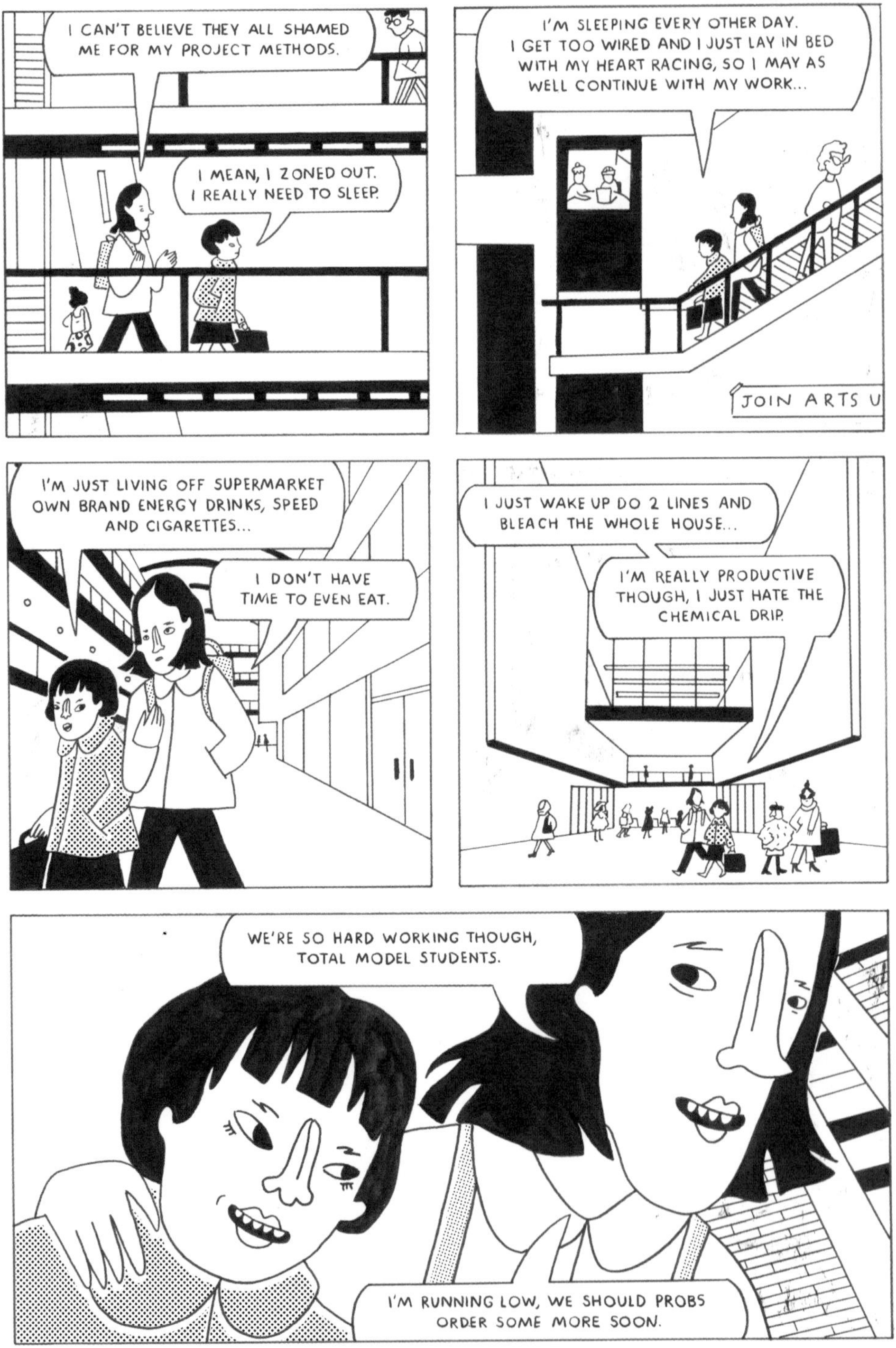
I CAN'T BELIEVE THEY ALL SHAMED ME FOR MY PROJECT METHODS.
I MEAN, I ZONED OUT. I REALLY NEED TO SLEEP.
I'M SLEEPING EVERY OTHER DAY. I GET TOO WIRED AND I JUST LAY IN BED WITH MY HEART RACING, SO I MAY AS WELL CONTINUE WITH MY WORK...
JOIN ARTS U
I'M JUST LIVING OFF SUPERMARKET OWN BRAND ENERGY DRINKS, SPEED AND CIGARETTES...
I DON'T HAVE TIME TO EVEN EAT.
I JUST WAKE UP DO 2 LINES AND BLEACH THE WHOLE HOUSE...
I'M REALLY PRODUCTIVE THOUGH, I JUST HATE THE CHEMICAL DRIP.
WE'RE SO HARD WORKING THOUGH, TOTAL MODEL STUDENTS.
I'M RUNNING LOW, WE SHOULD PROBS ORDER SOME MORE SOON.

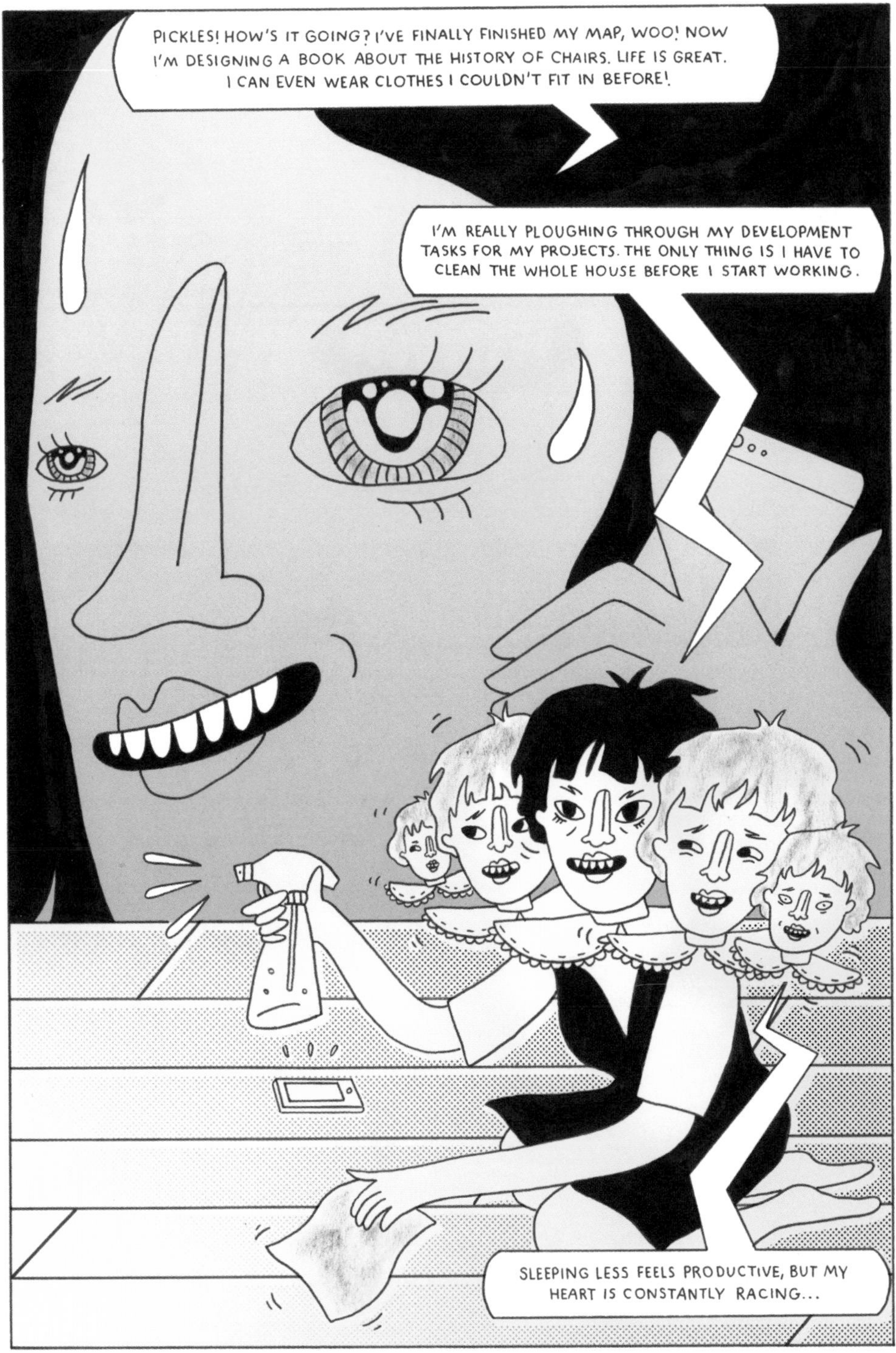
PICKLES! HOW'S IT GOING? I'VE FINALLY FINISHED MY MAP, WOO! NOW I'M DESIGNING A BOOK ABOUT THE HISTORY OF CHAIRS. LIFE IS GREAT. I CAN EVEN WEAR CLOTHES I COULDN'T FIT IN BEFORE!
I'M REALLY PLOUGHING THROUGH MY DEVELOPMENT TASKS FOR MY PROJECTS. THE ONLY THING IS I HAVE TO CLEAN THE WHOLE HOUSE BEFORE I START WORKING.
SLEEPING LESS FEELS PRODUCTIVE, BUT MY HEART IS CONSTANTLY RACING...

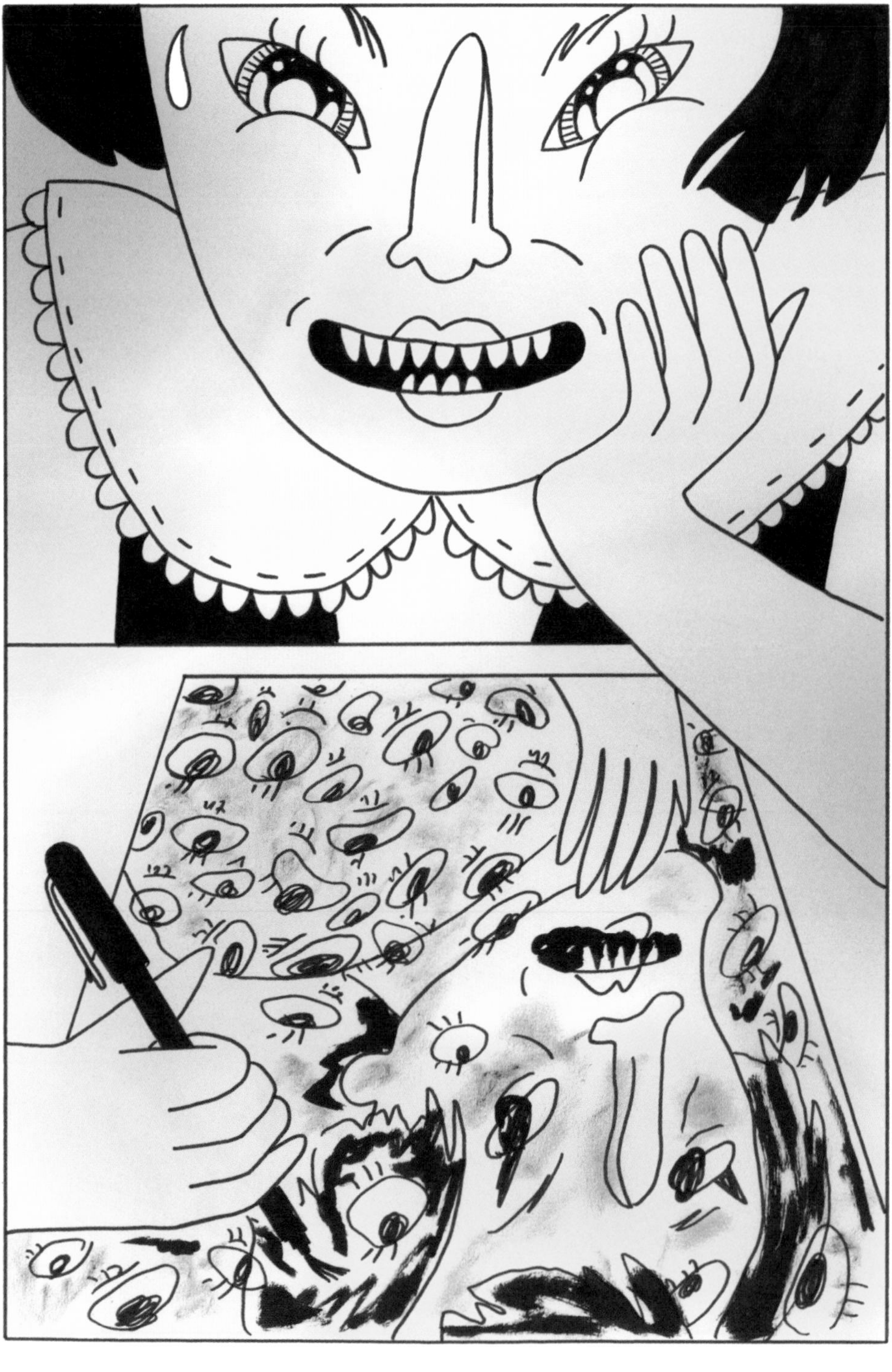

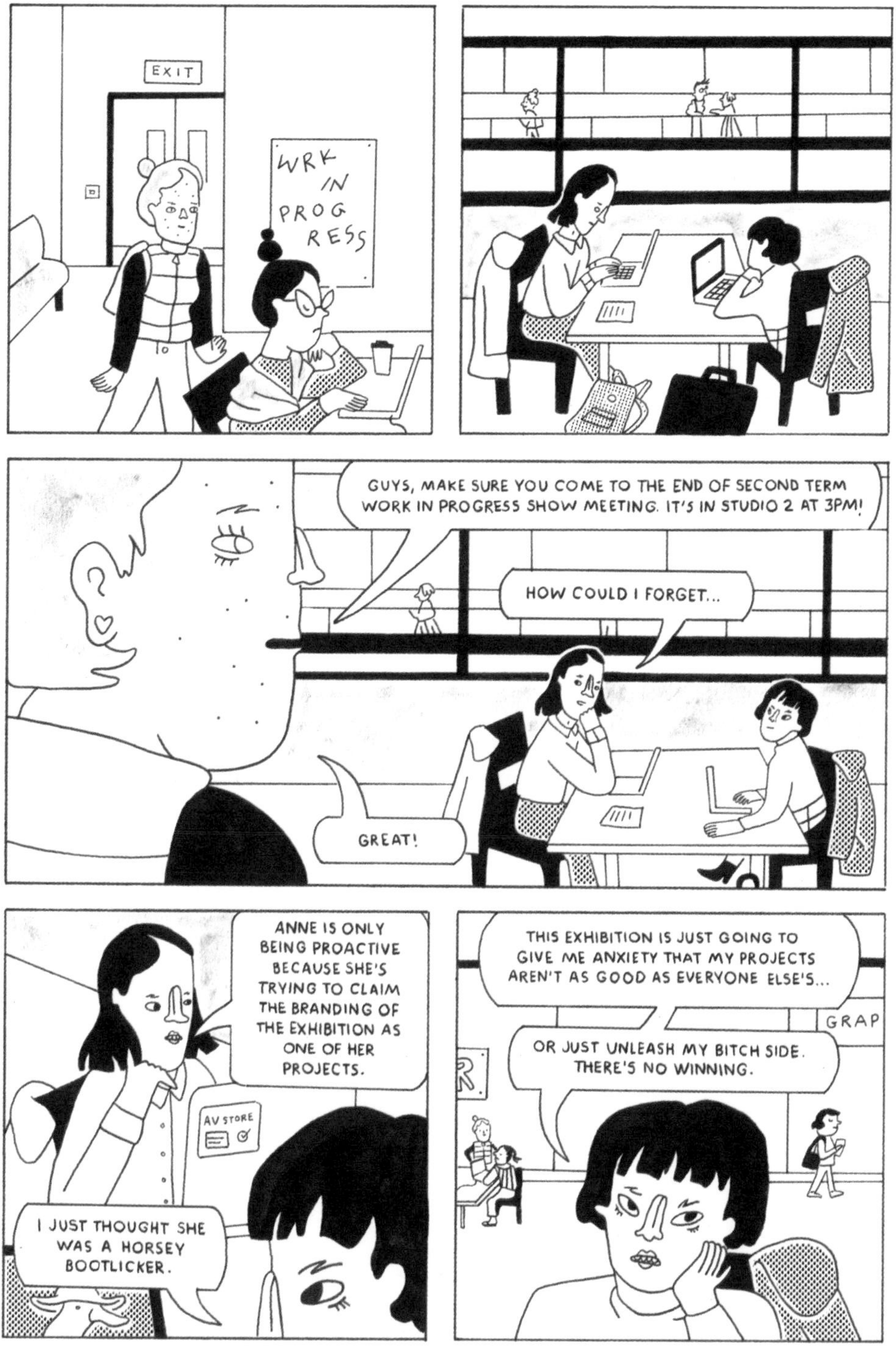
EXIT
WRK IN PROGRESS
GUYS, MAKE SURE YOU COME TO THE END OF SECOND TERM WORK IN PROGRESS SHOW MEETING. IT'S IN STUDIO 2 AT 3PM!
HOW COULD I FORGET...
GREAT!
ANNE IS ONLY BEING PROACTIVE BECAUSE SHE'S TRYING TO CLAIM THE BRANDING OF THE EXHIBITION AS ONE OF HER PROJECTS.
AV STORE
I JUST THOUGHT SHE WAS A HORSEY BOOTLICKER.
THIS EXHIBITION IS JUST GOING TO GIVE ME ANXIETY THAT MY PROJECTS AREN'T AS GOOD AS EVERYONE ELSE'S...
GRAP
OR JUST UNLEASH MY BITCH SIDE. THERE'S NO WINNING.

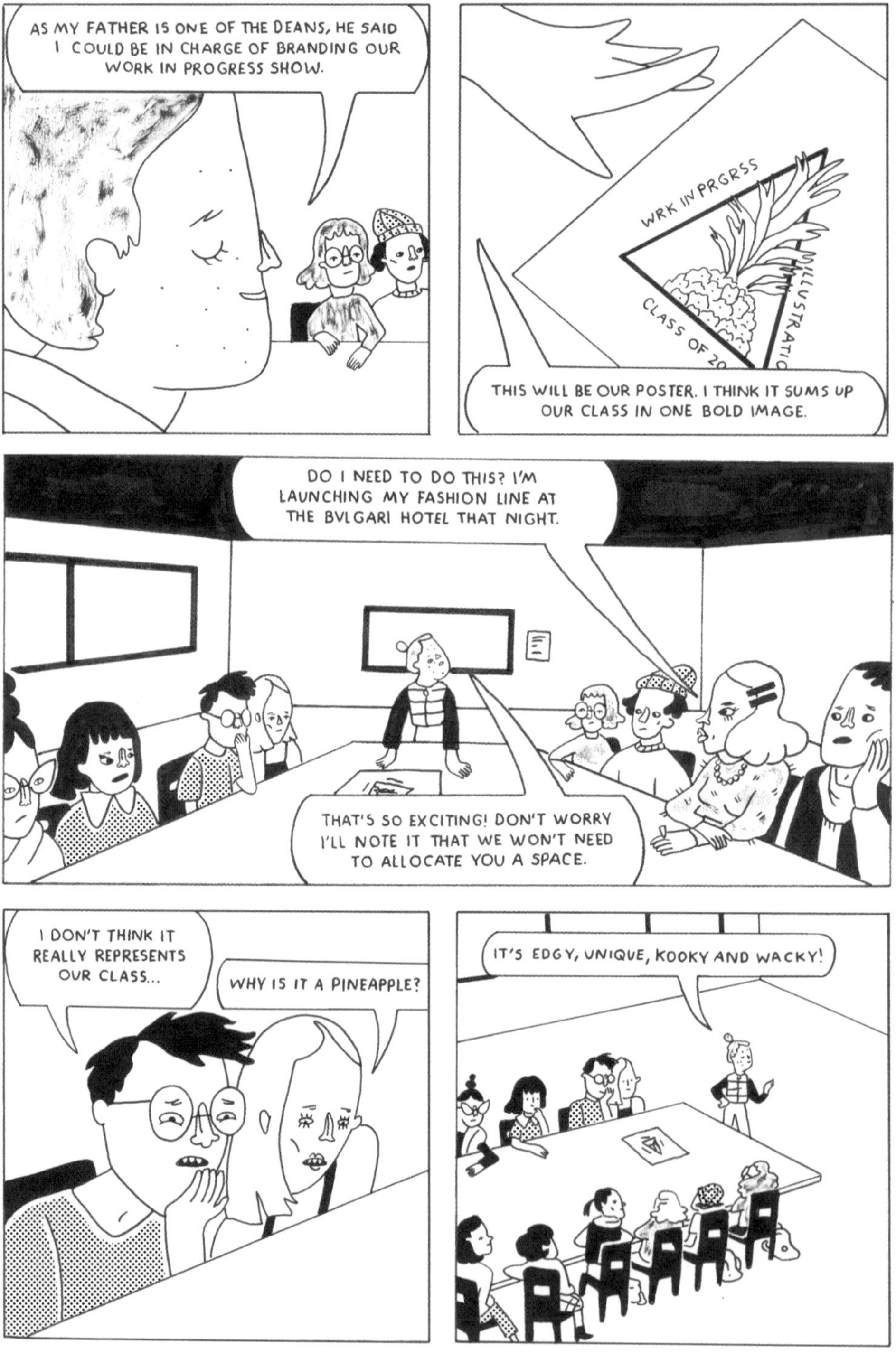
AS MY FATHER IS ONE OF THE DEANS, HE SAID I COULD BE IN CHARGE OF BRANDING OUR WORK IN PROGRESS SHOW.
WRK IN PRGRSS
ILLUSTRATIO
CLASS OF 20
THIS WILL BE OUR POSTER. I THINK IT SUMS UP OUR CLASS IN ONE BOLD IMAGE.
DO I NEED TO DO THIS? I'M LAUNCHING MY FASHION LINE AT THE BVLGARI HOTEL THAT NIGHT.
THAT'S SO EXCITING! DON'T WORRY I'LL NOTE IT THAT WE WON'T NEED TO ALLOCATE YOU A SPACE.
I DON'T THINK IT REALLY REPRESENTS OUR CLASS...
WHY IS IT A PINEAPPLE?
IT'S EDGY, UNIQUE, KOOKY AND WACKY!

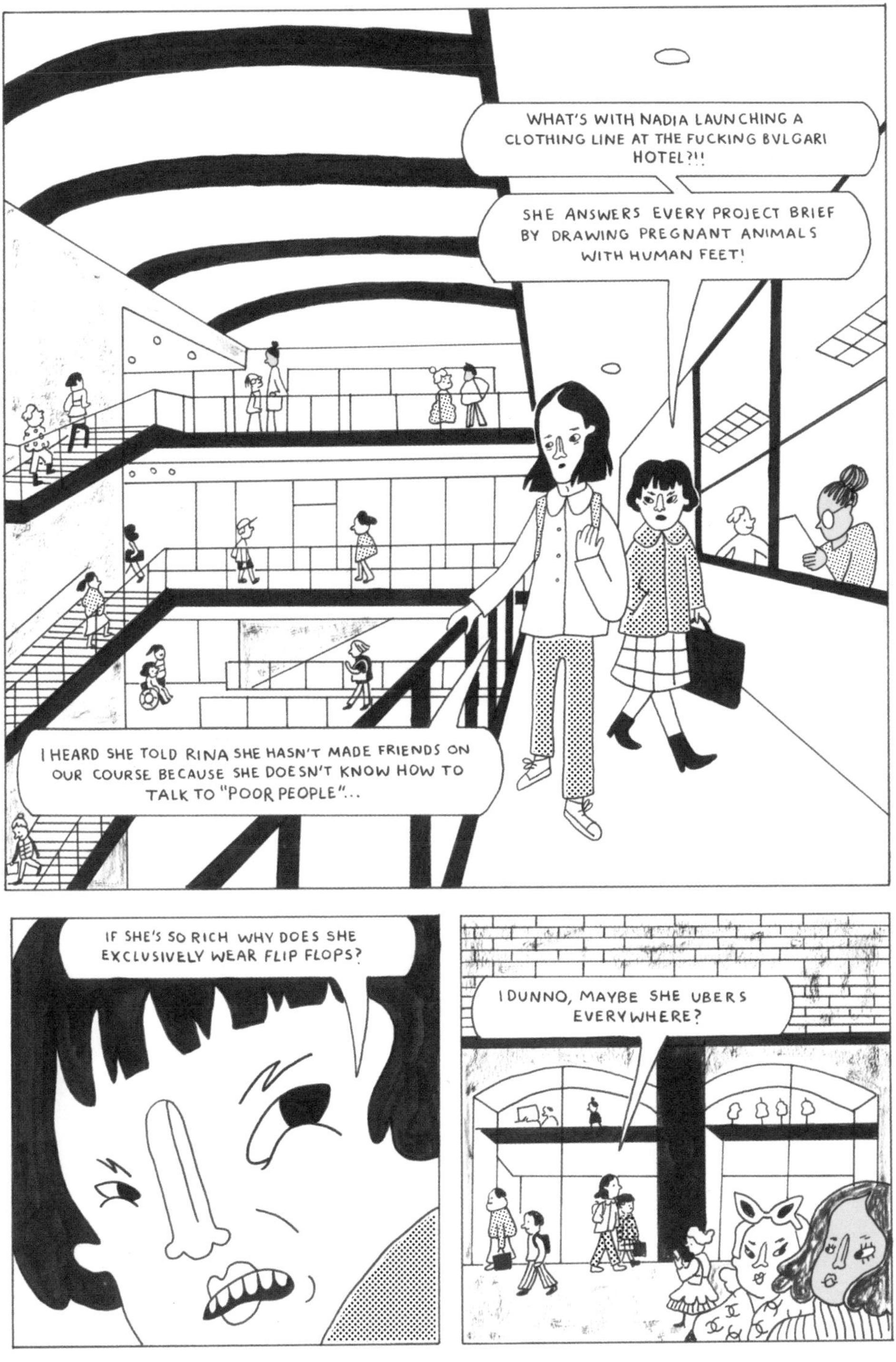
WHAT'S WITH NADIA LAUNCHING A CLOTHING LINE AT THE FUCKING BVLGARI HOTEL?!!
SHE ANSWERS EVERY PROJECT BRIEF BY DRAWING PREGNANT ANIMALS WITH HUMAN FEET!
I HEARD SHE TOLD RINA SHE HASN'T MADE FRIENDS ON OUR COURSE BECAUSE SHE DOESN'T KNOW HOW TO TALK TO "POOR PEOPLE"...
IF SHE'S SO RICH WHY DOES SHE EXCLUSIVELY WEAR FLIP FLOPS?
I DUNNO, MAYBE SHE UBERS EVERYWHERE?

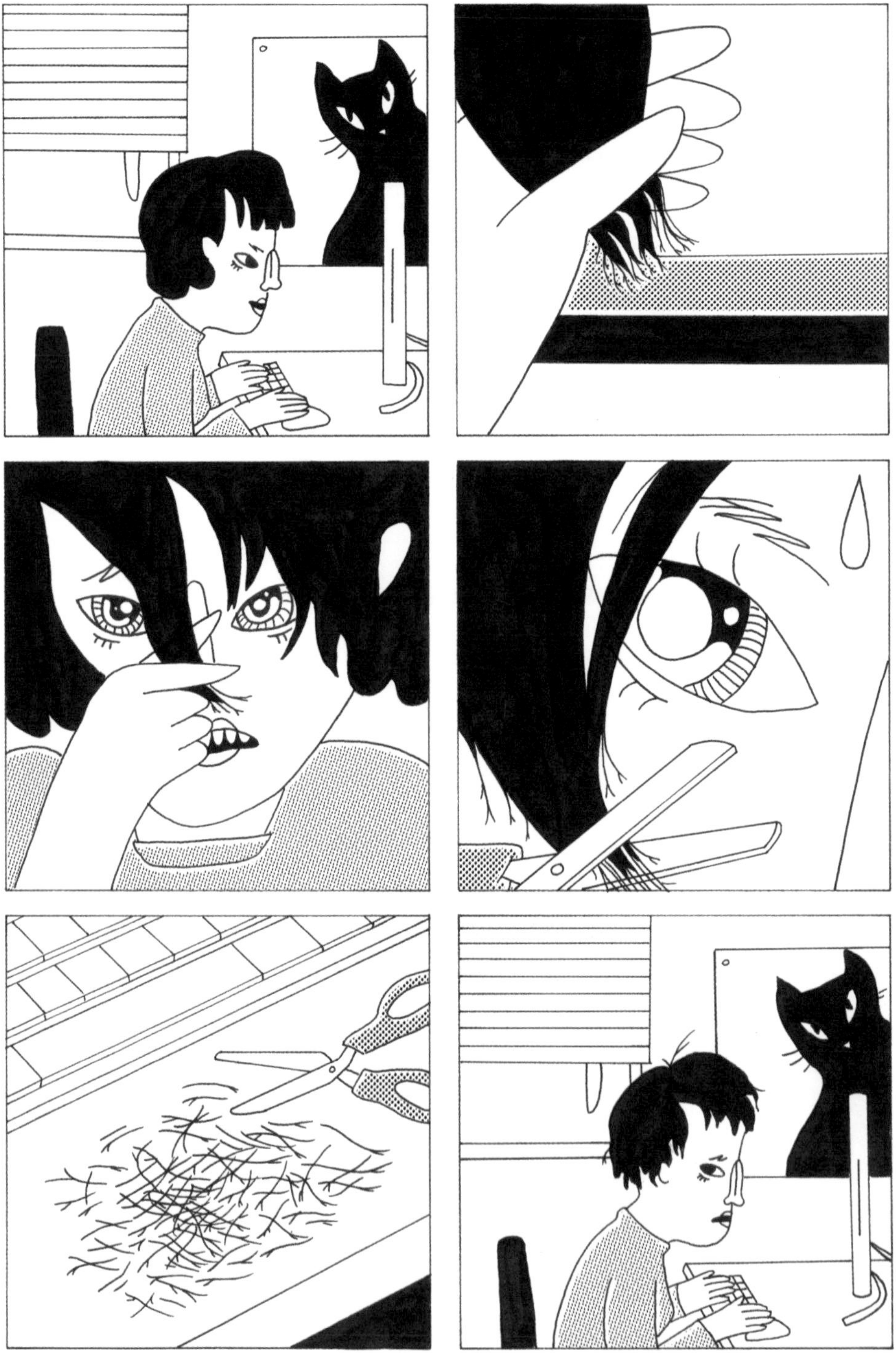

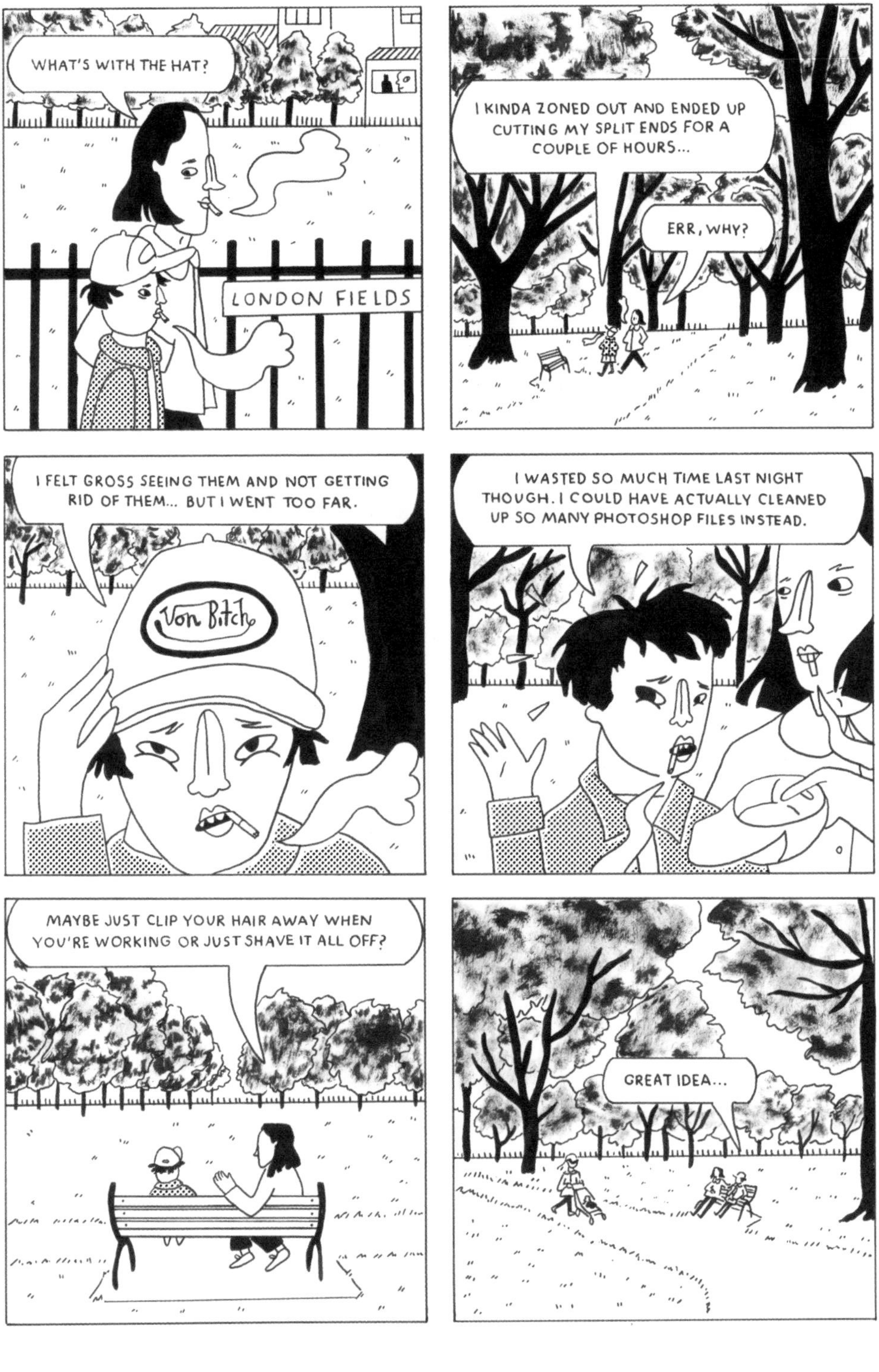
WHAT'S WITH THE HAT?
LONDON FIELDS
I KINDA ZONED OUT AND ENDED UP CUTTING MY SPLIT ENDS FOR A COUPLE OF HOURS...
ERR, WHY?
I FELT GROSS SEEING THEM AND NOT GETTING RID OF THEM... BUT I WENT TOO FAR.
Von Bitch
I WASTED SO MUCH TIME LAST NIGHT THOUGH. I COULD HAVE ACTUALLY CLEANED UP SO MANY PHOTOSHOP FILES INSTEAD.
MAYBE JUST CLIP YOUR HAIR AWAY WHEN YOU'RE WORKING OR JUST SHAVE IT ALL OFF?
GREAT IDEA...

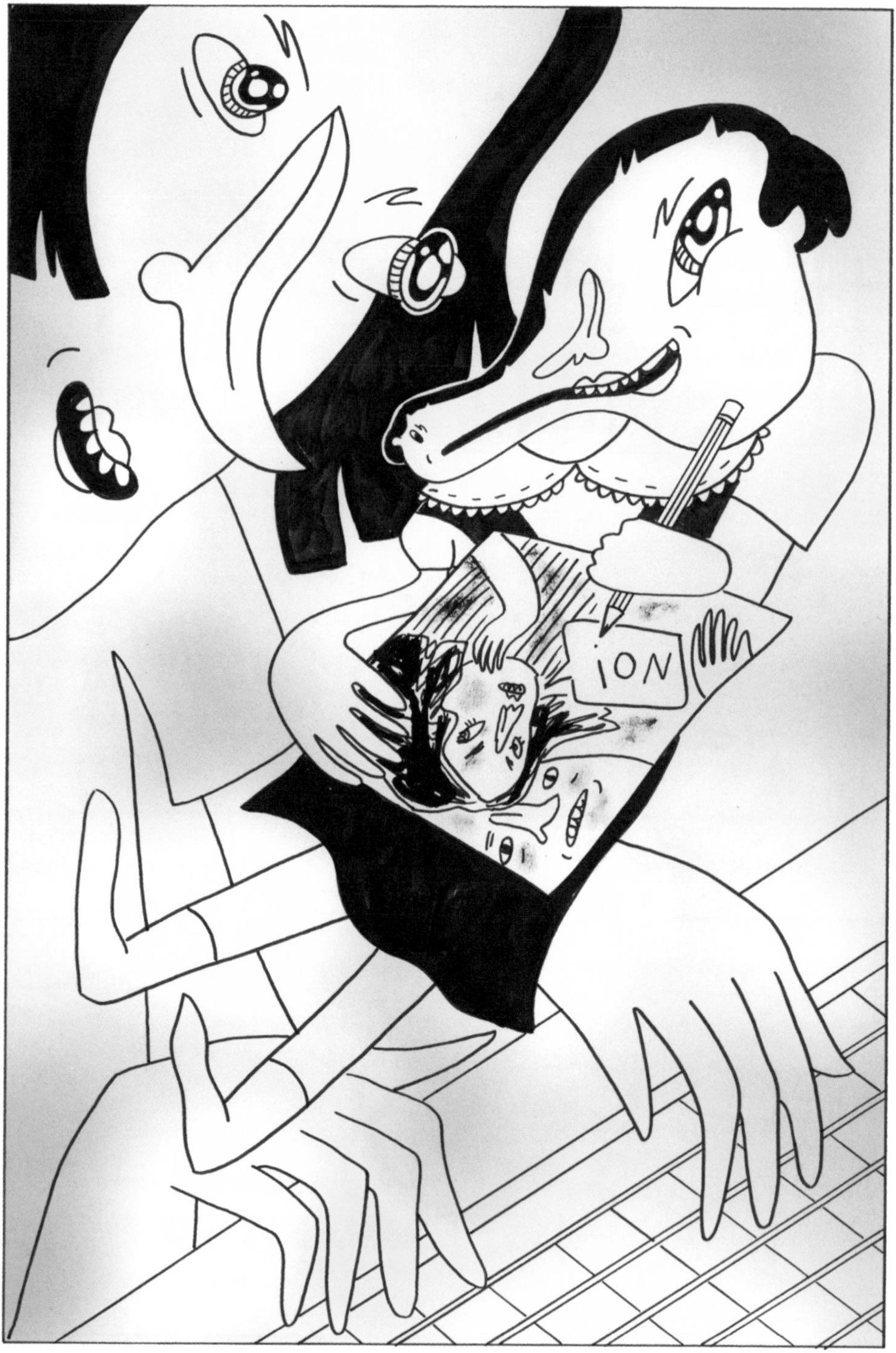
ION

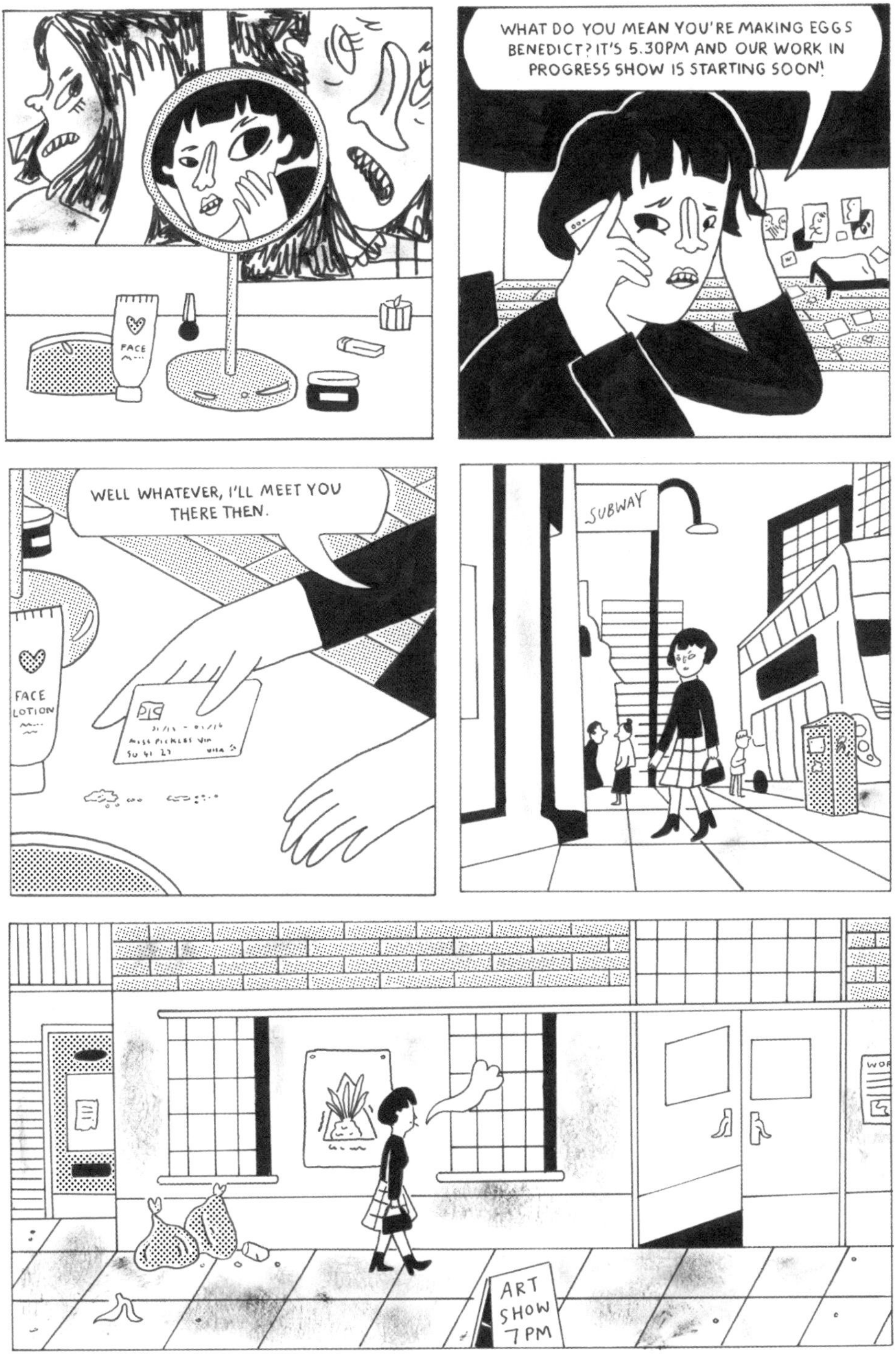
FACE
WHAT DO YOU MEAN YOU'RE MAKING EGGS BENEDICT? IT'S 5.30PM AND OUR WORK IN PROGRESS SHOW IS STARTING SOON!
WELL WHATEVER, I'LL MEET YOU THERE THEN.
FACE LOTION
SUBWAY
ART SHOW 7PM

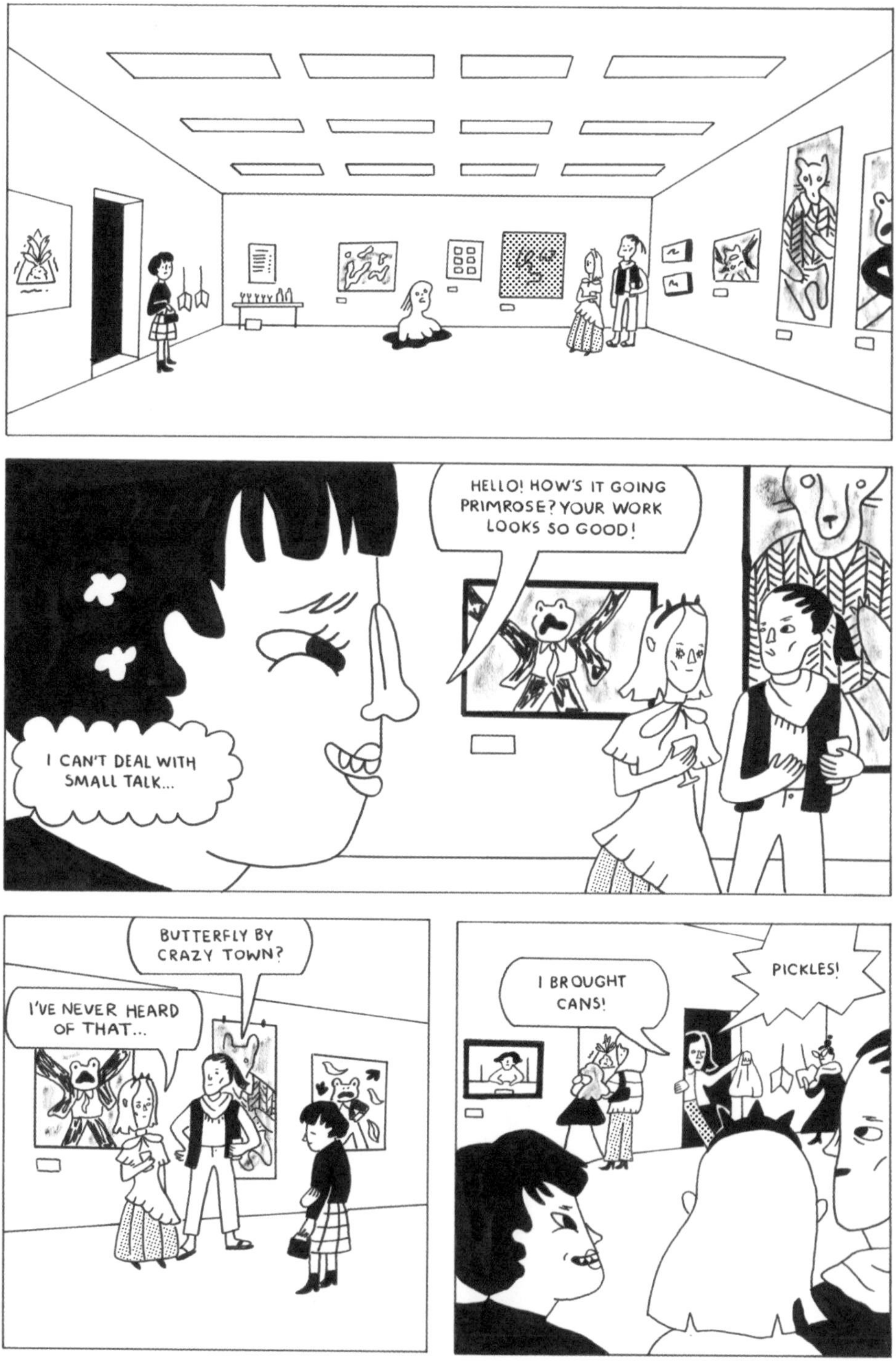
HELLO! HOW'S IT GOING PRIMROSE? YOUR WORK LOOKS SO GOOD!
I CAN'T DEAL WITH SMALL TALK...
BUTTERFLY BY CRAZY TOWN?
I'VE NEVER HEARD OF THAT...
I BROUGHT CANS!
PICKLES!

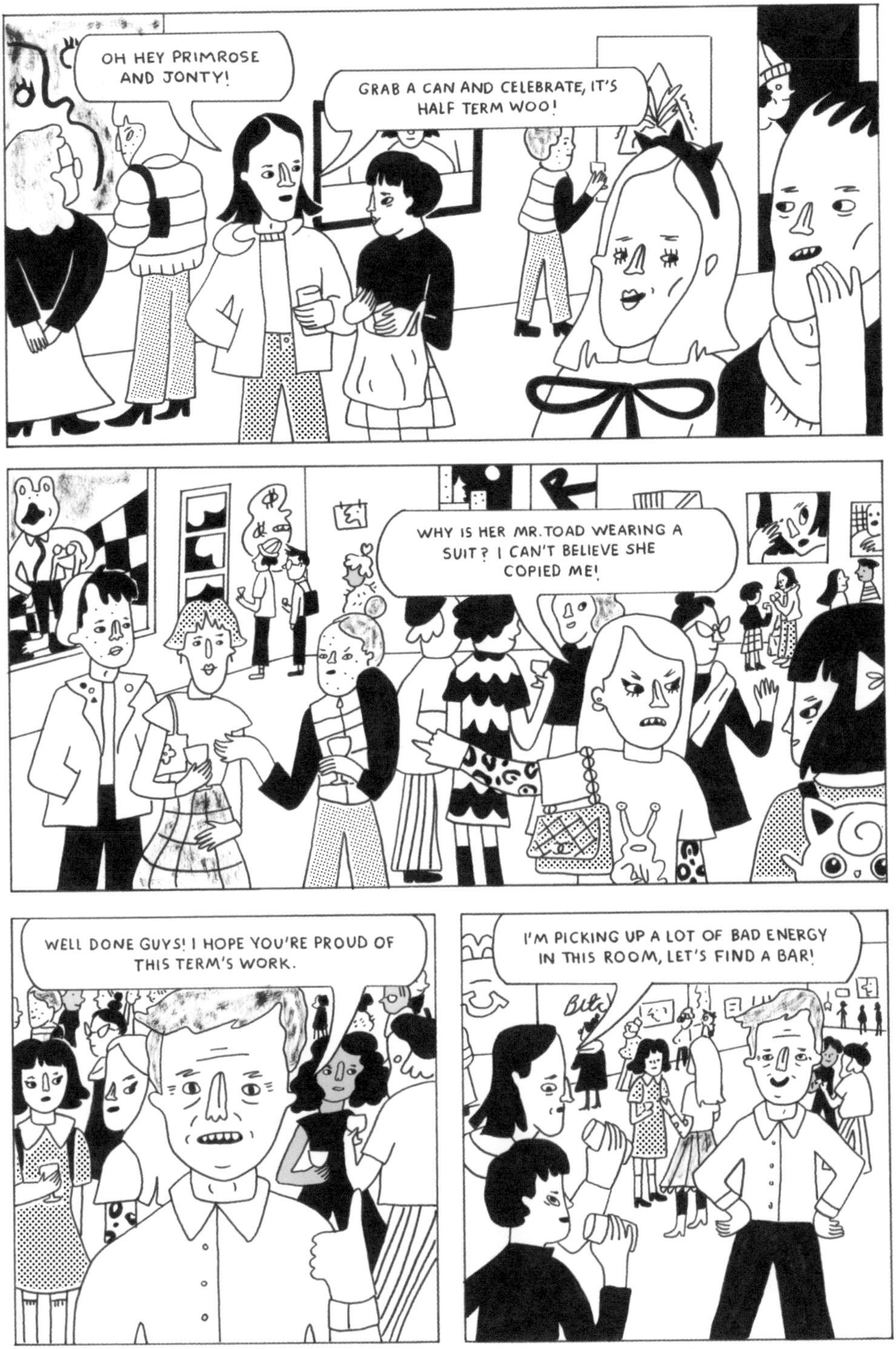
OH HEY PRIMROSE AND JONTY!
GRAB A CAN AND CELEBRATE, IT'S HALF TERM WOO!
WHY IS HER MR. TOAD WEARING A SUIT? I CAN'T BELIEVE SHE COPIED ME!
WELL DONE GUYS! I HOPE YOU'RE PROUD OF THIS TERM'S WORK.
I'M PICKING UP A LOT OF BAD ENERGY IN THIS ROOM, LET'S FIND A BAR!

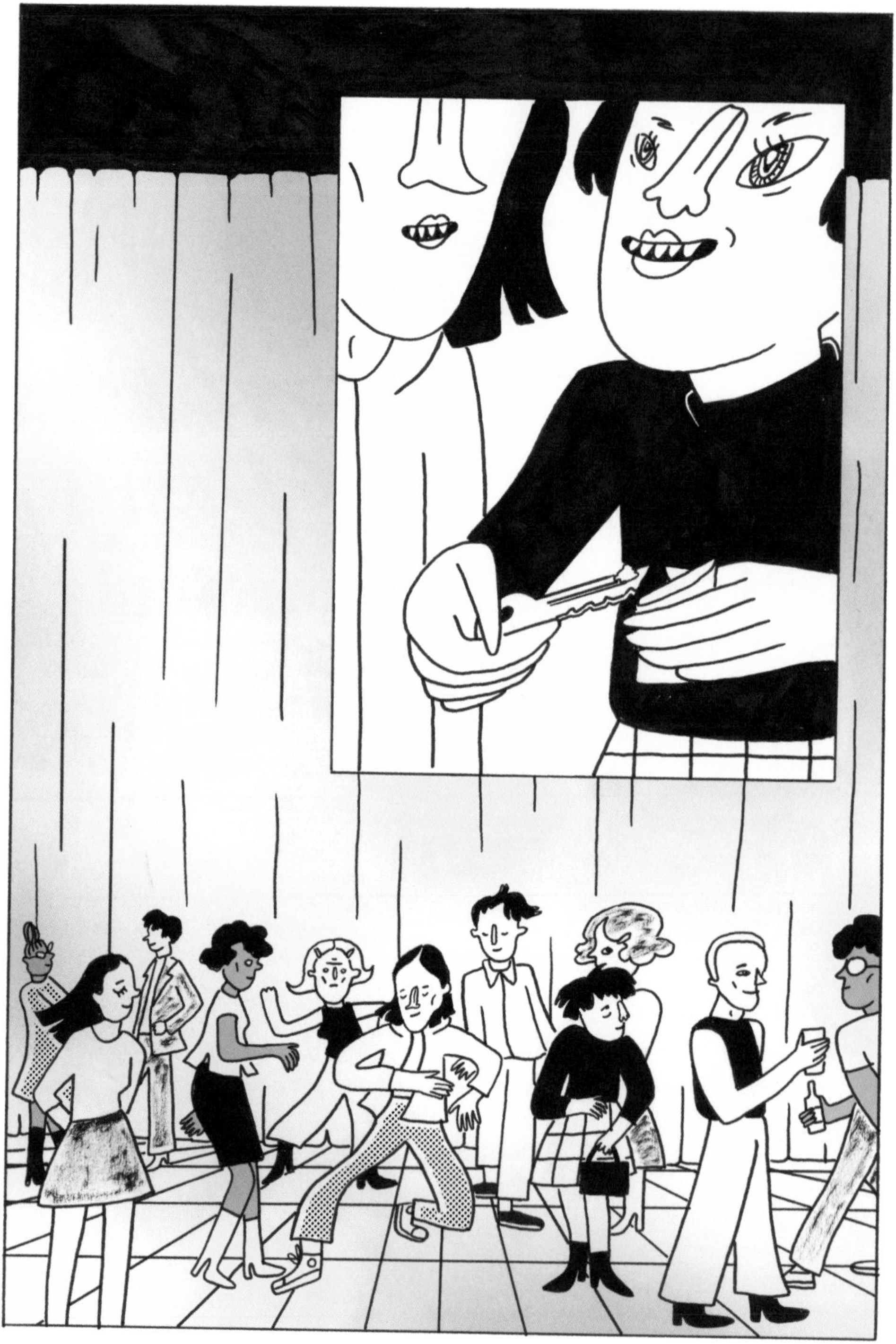

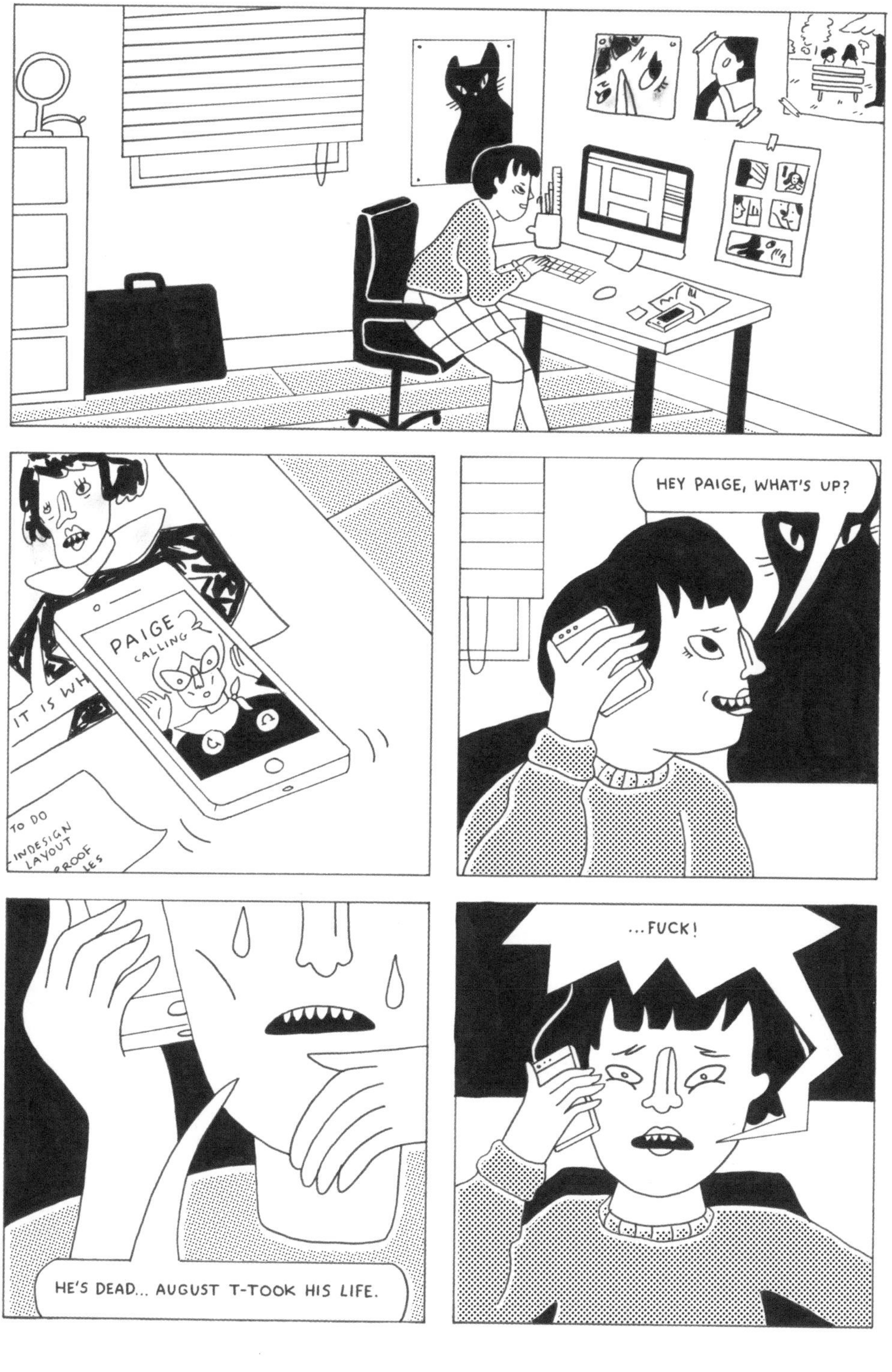
PAIGE CALLING
IT IS WH
TO DO
INDESIGN LAYOUT
PROOF
HEY PAIGE, WHAT'S UP?
HE'S DEAD... AUGUST T-TOOK HIS LIFE.
...FUCK!

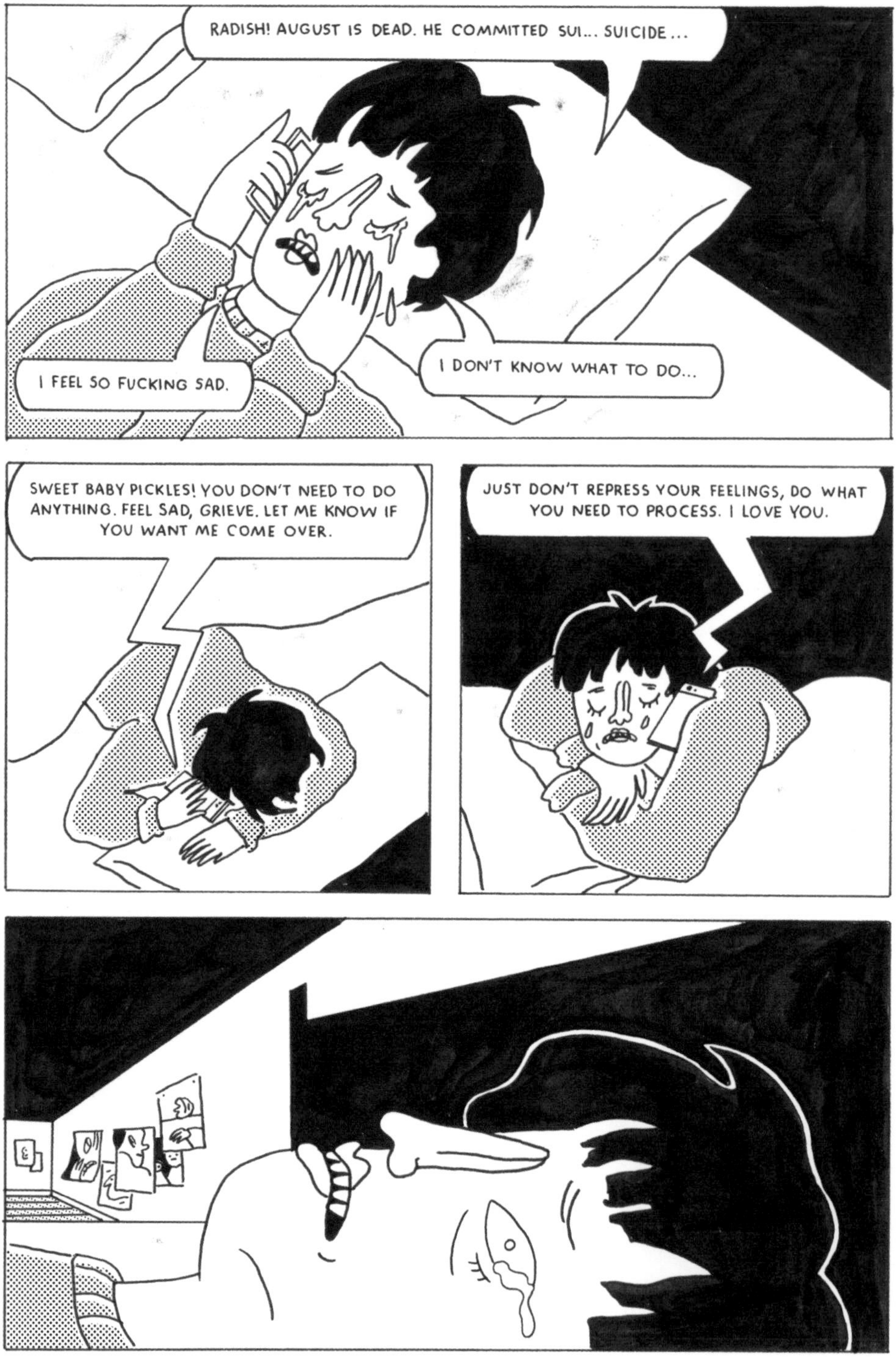
RADISH! AUGUST IS DEAD. HE COMMITTED SUI... SUICIDE...
I FEEL SO FUCKING SAD.
I DON'T KNOW WHAT TO DO...
SWEET BABY PICKLES! YOU DON'T NEED TO DO ANYTHING. FEEL SAD, GRIEVE. LET ME KNOW IF YOU WANT ME COME OVER.
JUST DON'T REPRESS YOUR FEELINGS, DO WHAT YOU NEED TO PROCESS. I LOVE YOU.

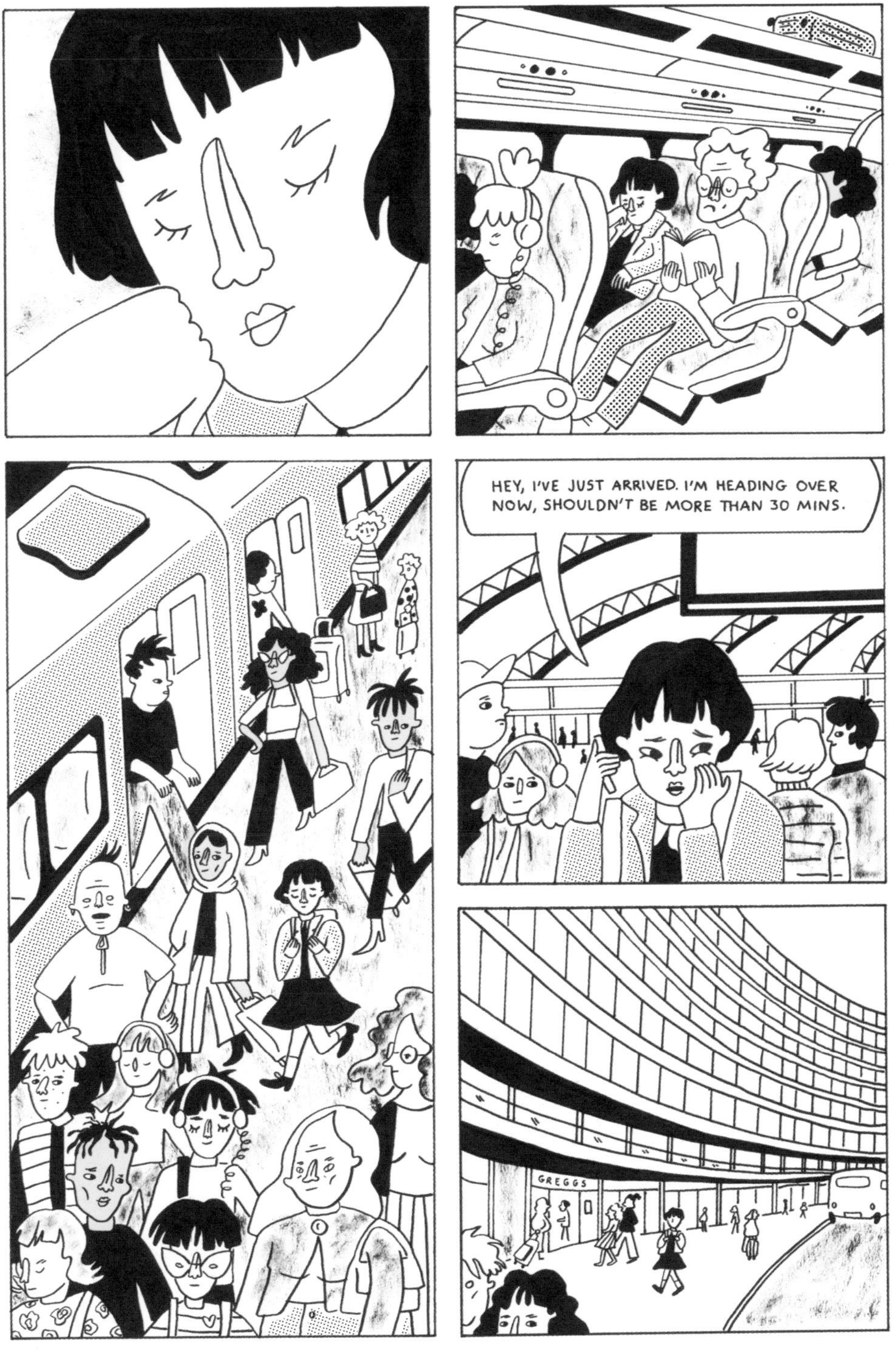
HEY, I'VE JUST ARRIVED. I'M HEADING OVER NOW, SHOULDN'T BE MORE THAN 30 MINS.
GREGGS

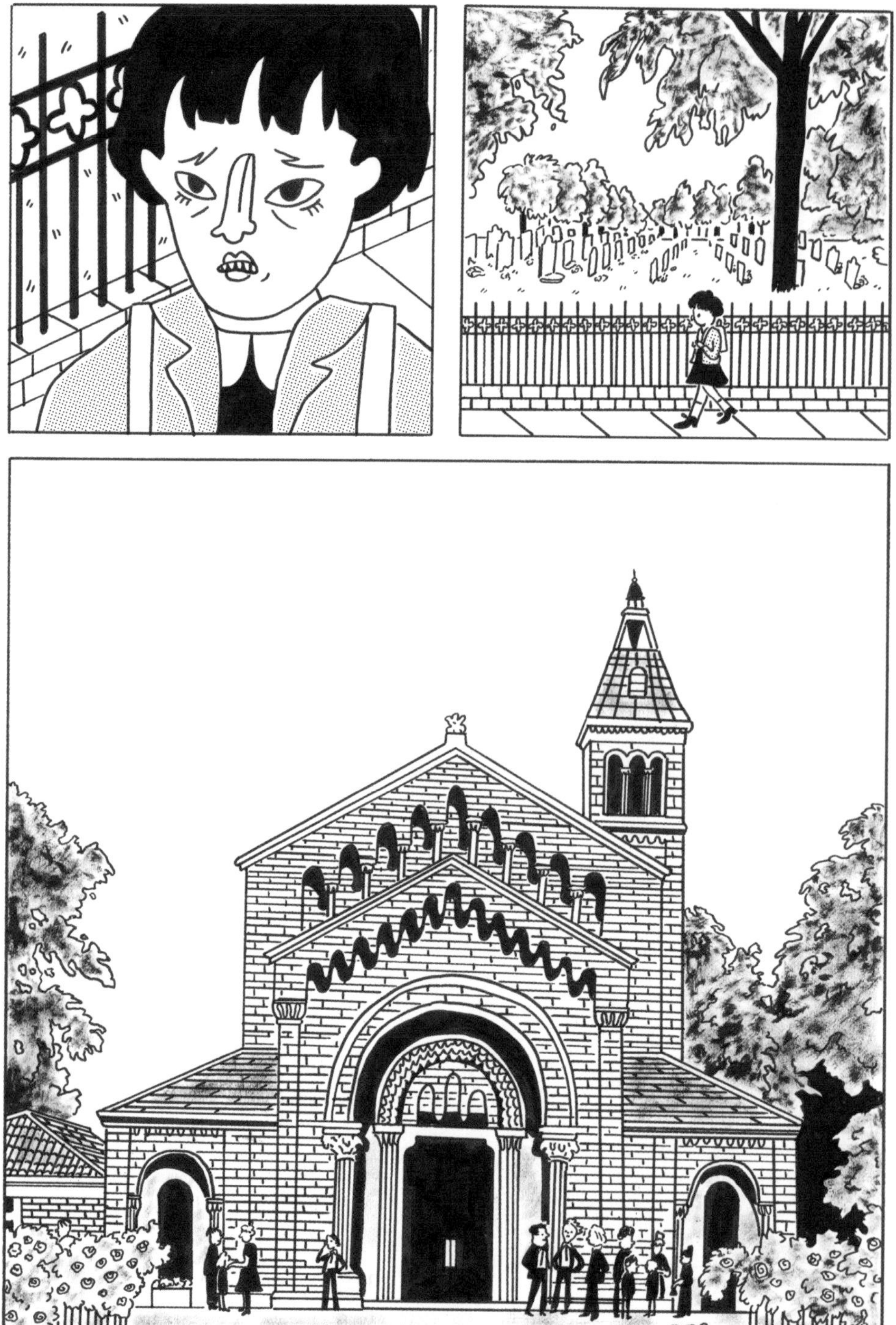

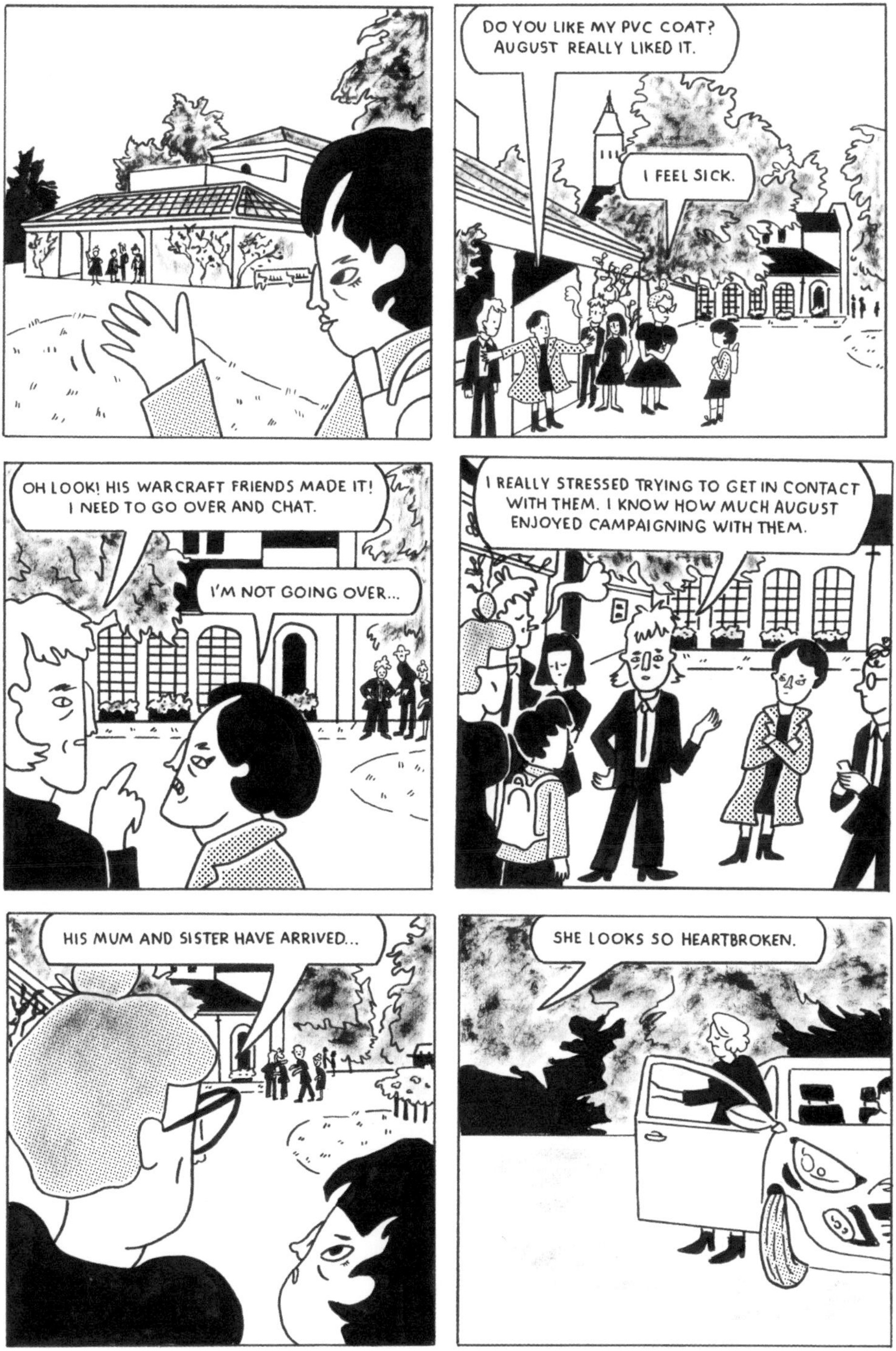
DO YOU LIKE MY PVC COAT? AUGUST REALLY LIKED IT.
I FEEL SICK.
OH LOOK! HIS WARCRAFT FRIENDS MADE IT! I NEED TO GO OVER AND CHAT.
I'M NOT GOING OVER...
I REALLY STRESSED TRYING TO GET IN CONTACT WITH THEM. I KNOW HOW MUCH AUGUST ENJOYED CAMPAIGNING WITH THEM.
HIS MUM AND SISTER HAVE ARRIVED...
SHE LOOKS SO HEARTBROKEN.

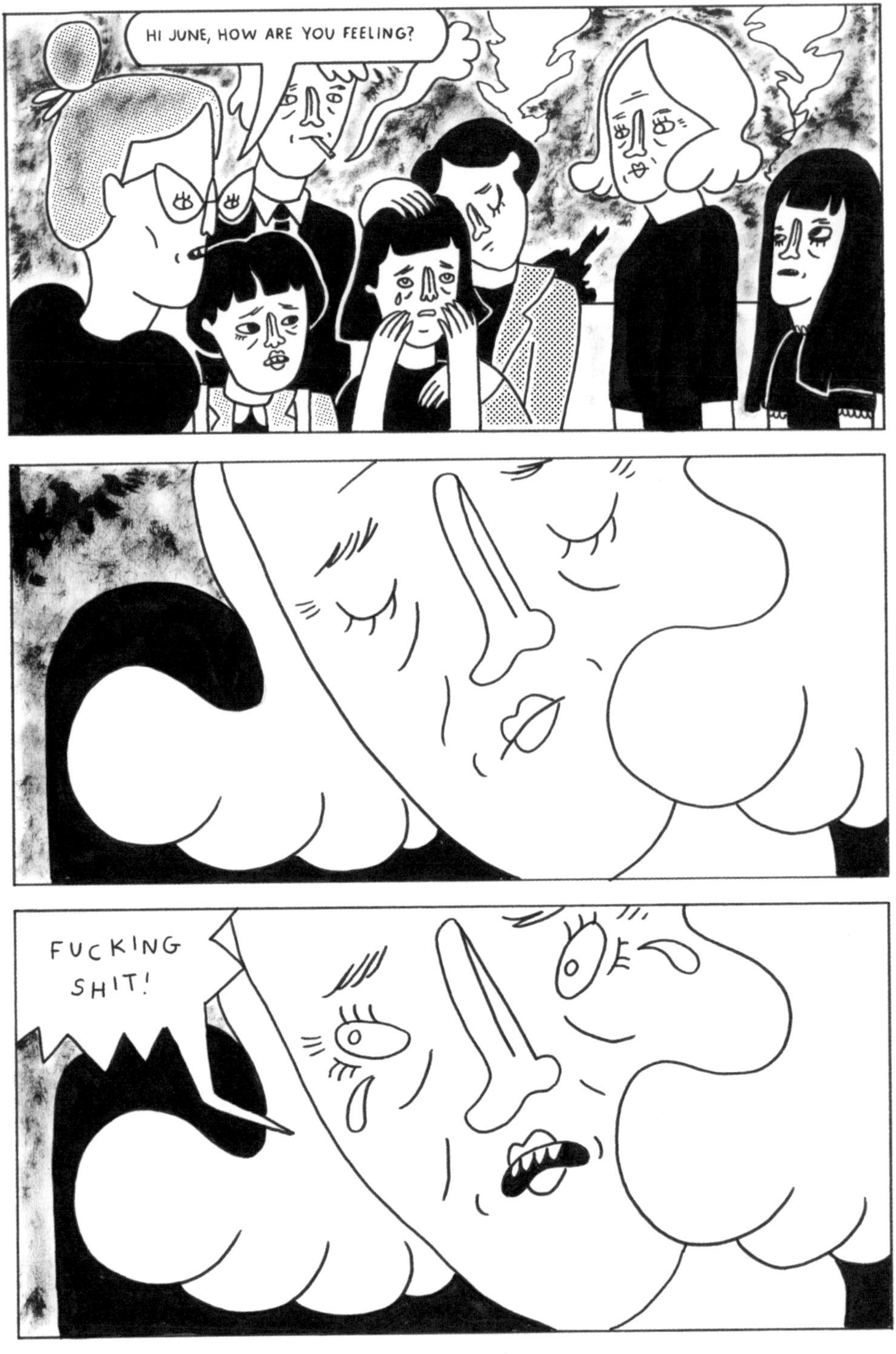
HI JUNE, HOW ARE YOU FEELING?
FUCKING SHIT!

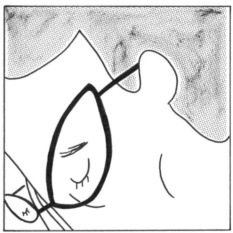

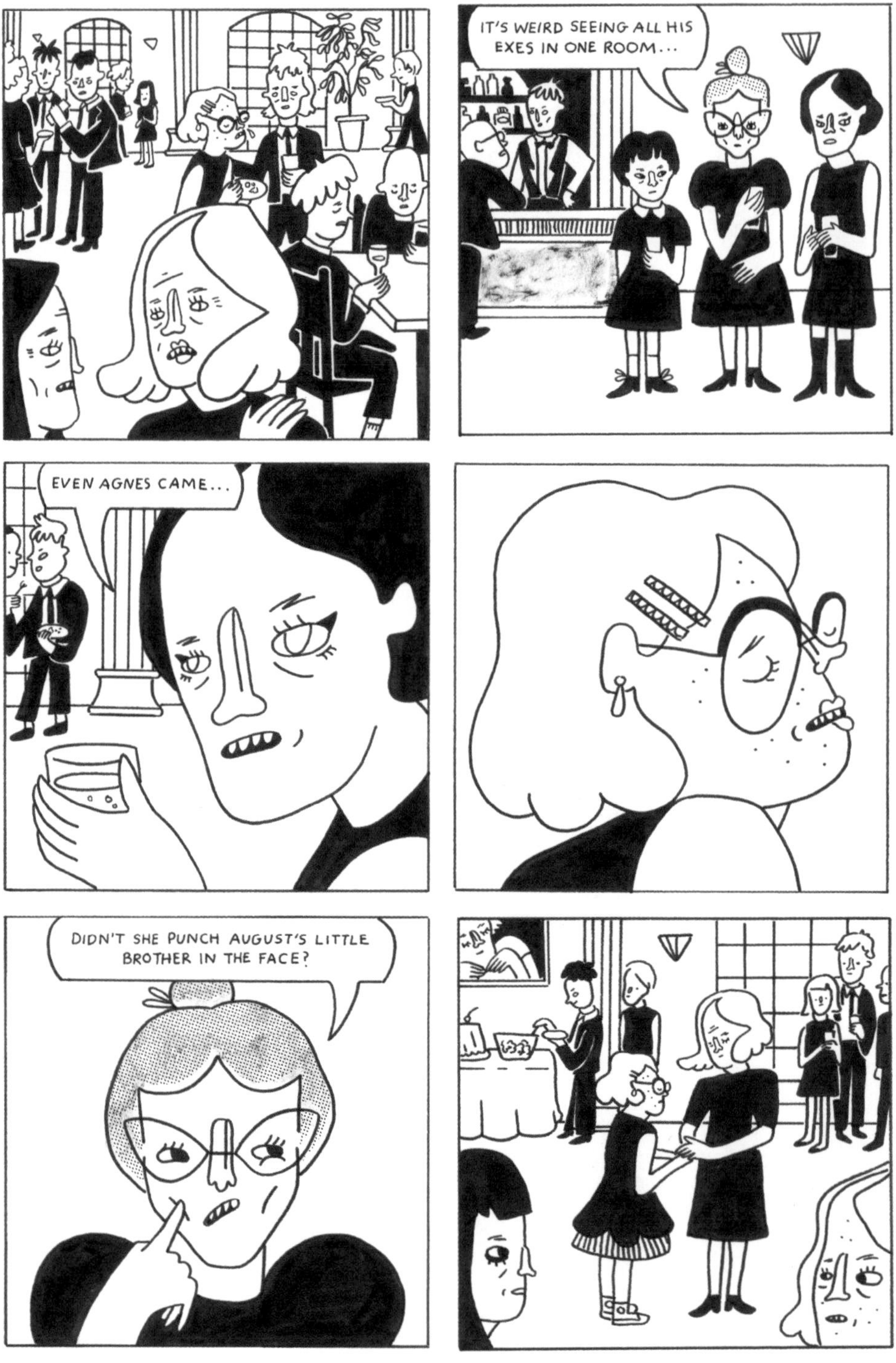
IT'S WEIRD SEEING ALL HIS EXES IN ONE ROOM...
EVEN AGNES CAME...
DIDN'T SHE PUNCH AUGUST'S LITTLE BROTHER IN THE FACE?

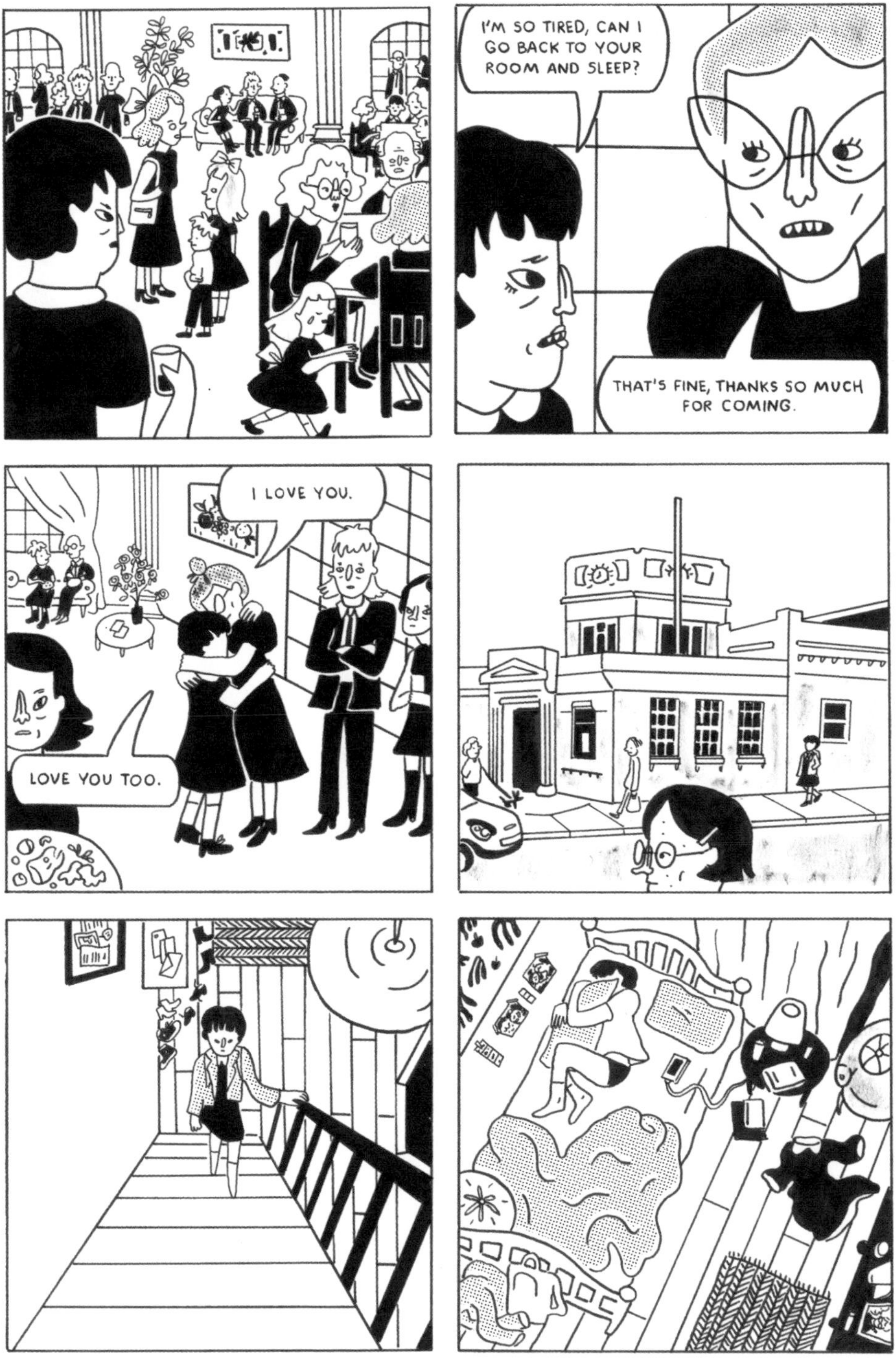

I'M SO TIRED, CAN I GO BACK TO YOUR ROOM AND SLEEP?
THAT'S FINE, THANKS SO MUCH FOR COMING.
I LOVE YOU.
LOVE YOU TOO.

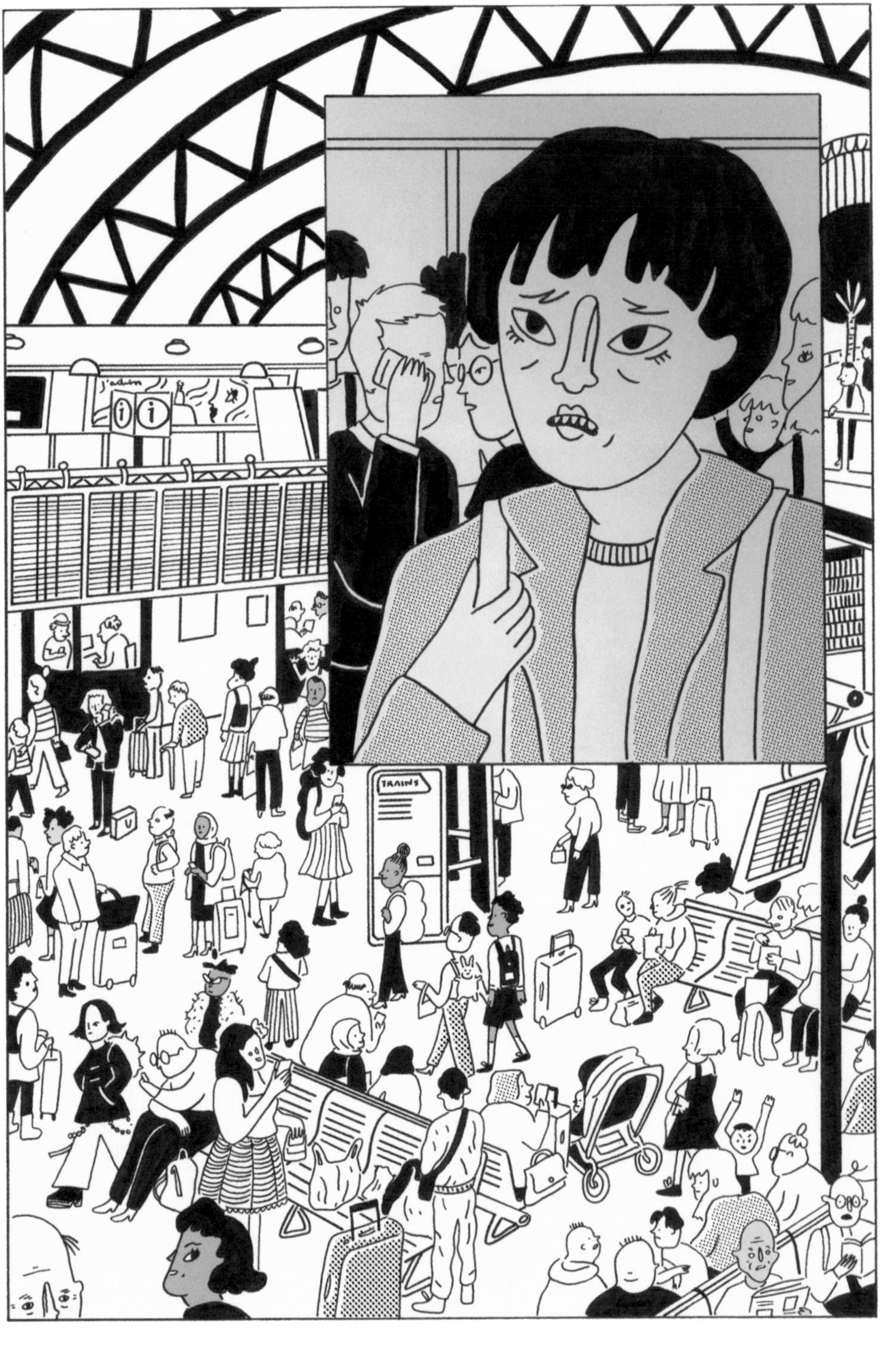
TRAINS

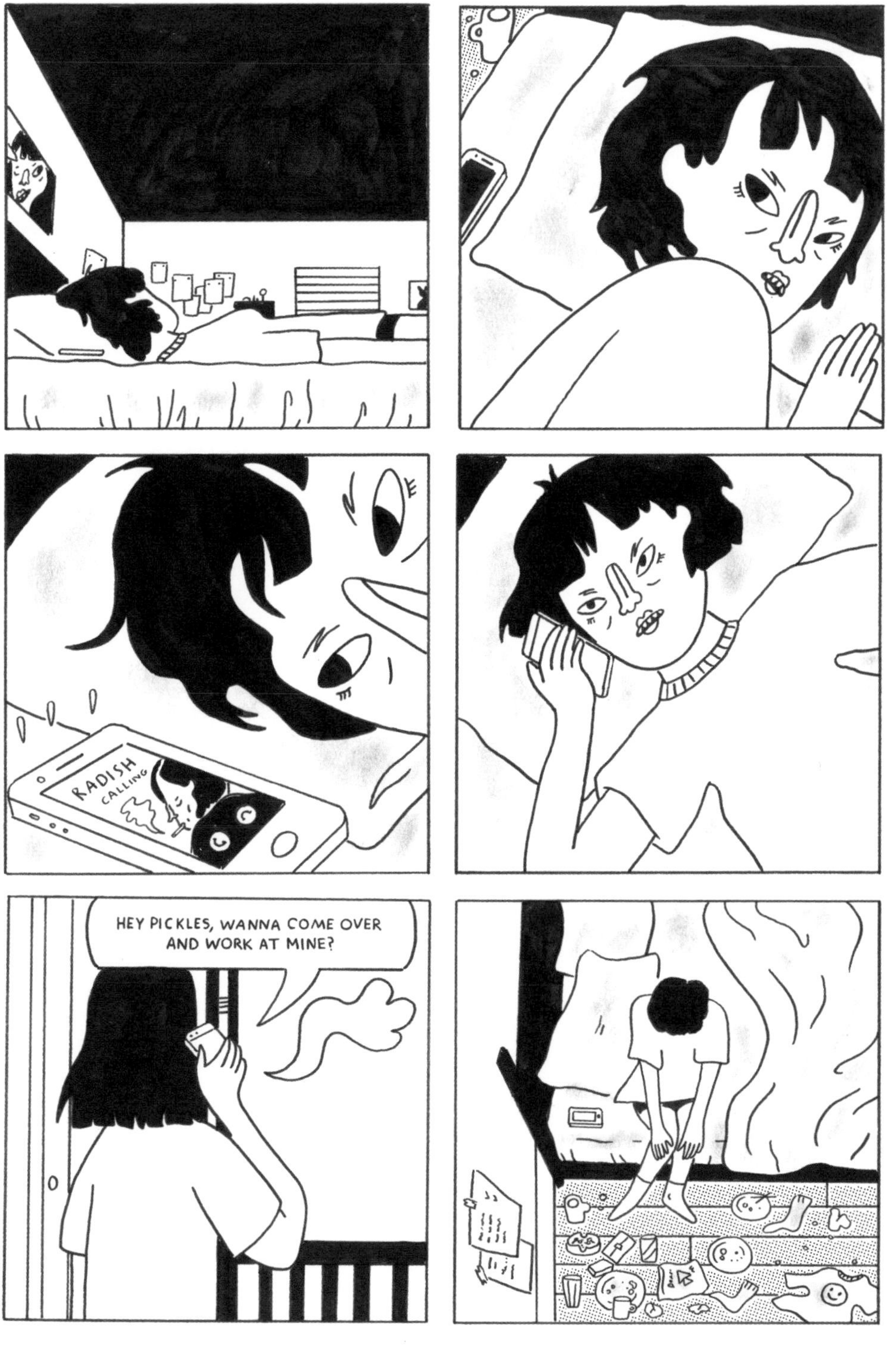
RADISH
CALLING
HEY PICKLES, WANNA COME OVER AND WORK AT MINE?

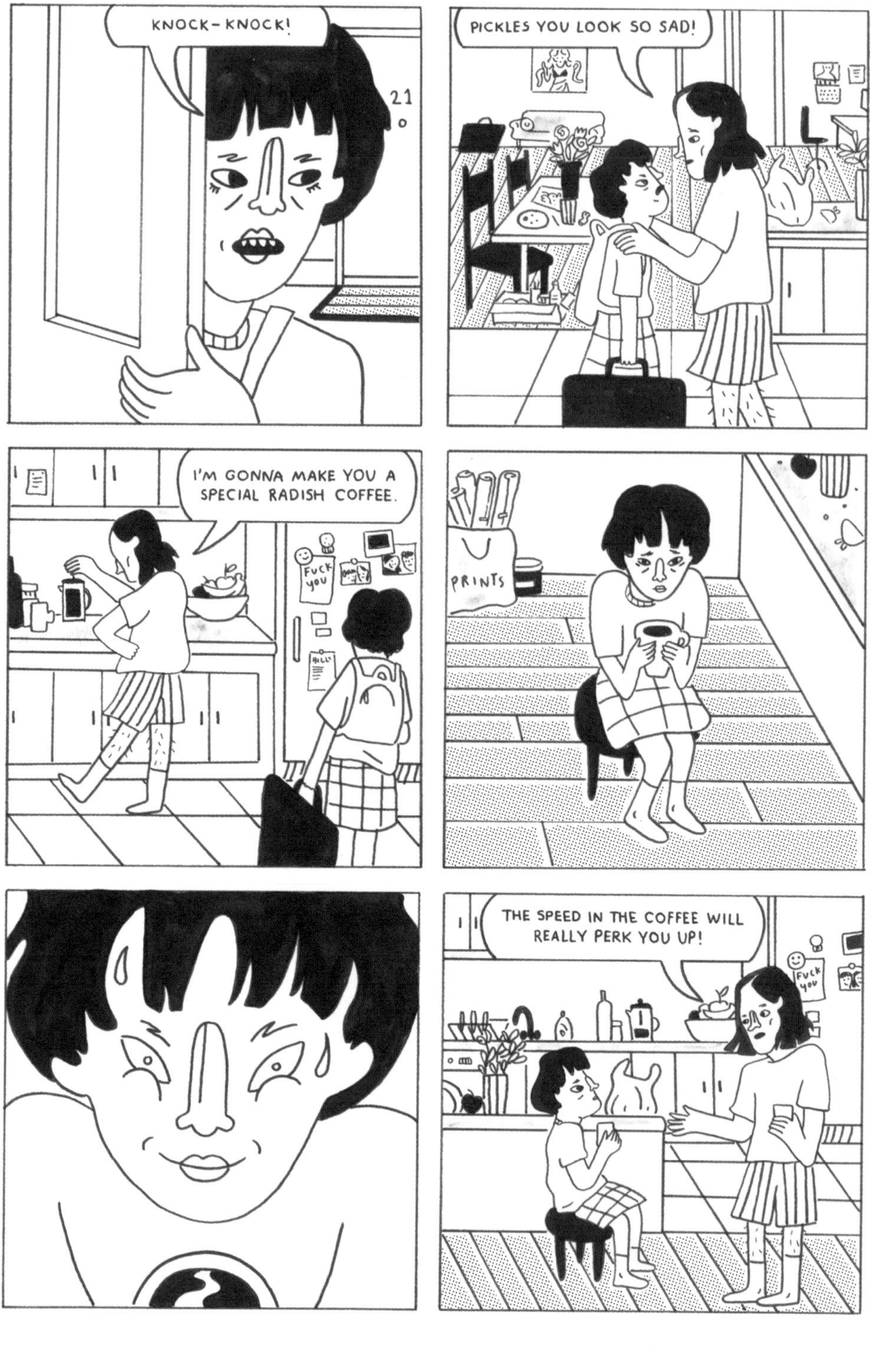
KNOCK-KNOCK!
21
PICKLES YOU LOOK SO SAD!
I'M GONNA MAKE YOU A SPECIAL RADISH COFFEE.
FUCK YOU
BILLS
PRINTS
THE SPEED IN THE COFFEE WILL REALLY PERK YOU UP!
FUCK YOU

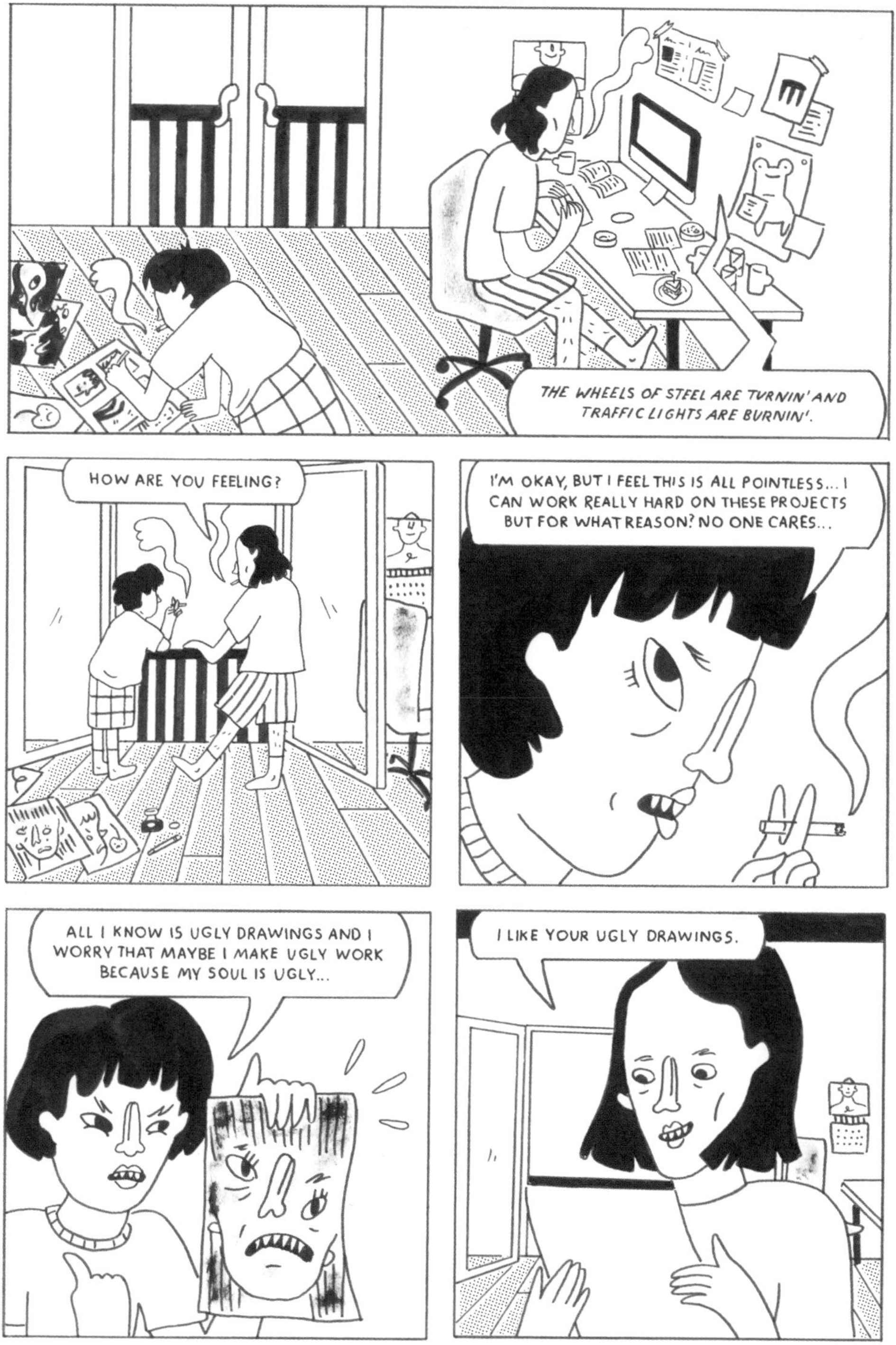
THE WHEELS OF STEEL ARE TURNIN' AND TRAFFIC LIGHTS ARE BURNIN'.
HOW ARE YOU FEELING?
I'M OKAY, BUT I FEEL THIS IS ALL POINTLESS... I CAN WORK REALLY HARD ON THESE PROJECTS BUT FOR WHAT REASON? NO ONE CARES...
ALL I KNOW IS UGLY DRAWINGS AND I WORRY THAT MAYBE I MAKE UGLY WORK BECAUSE MY SOUL IS UGLY...
I LIKE YOUR UGLY DRAWINGS.

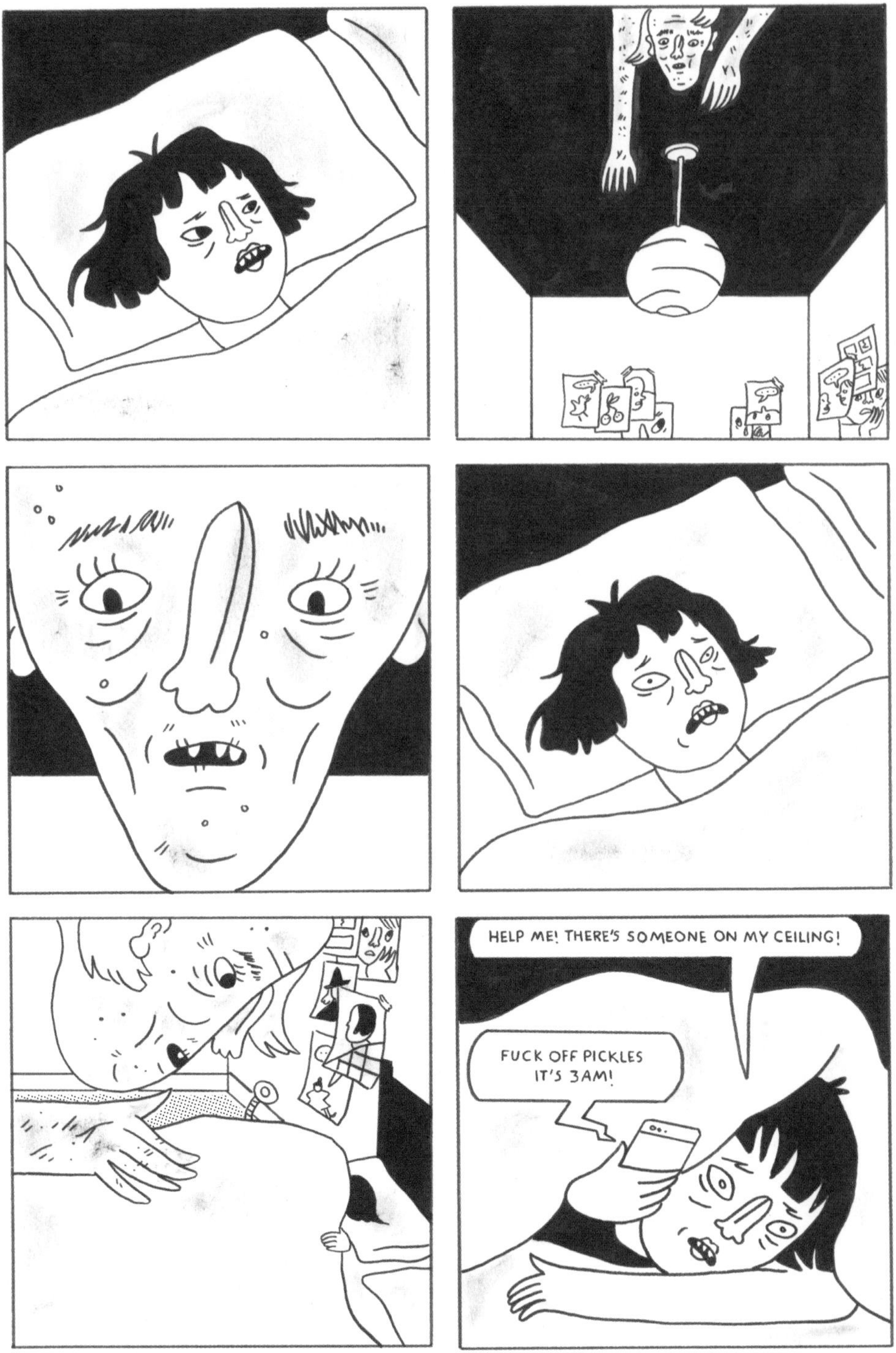
HELP ME! THERE'S SOMEONE ON MY CEILING!
FUCK OFF PICKLES IT'S 3AM!

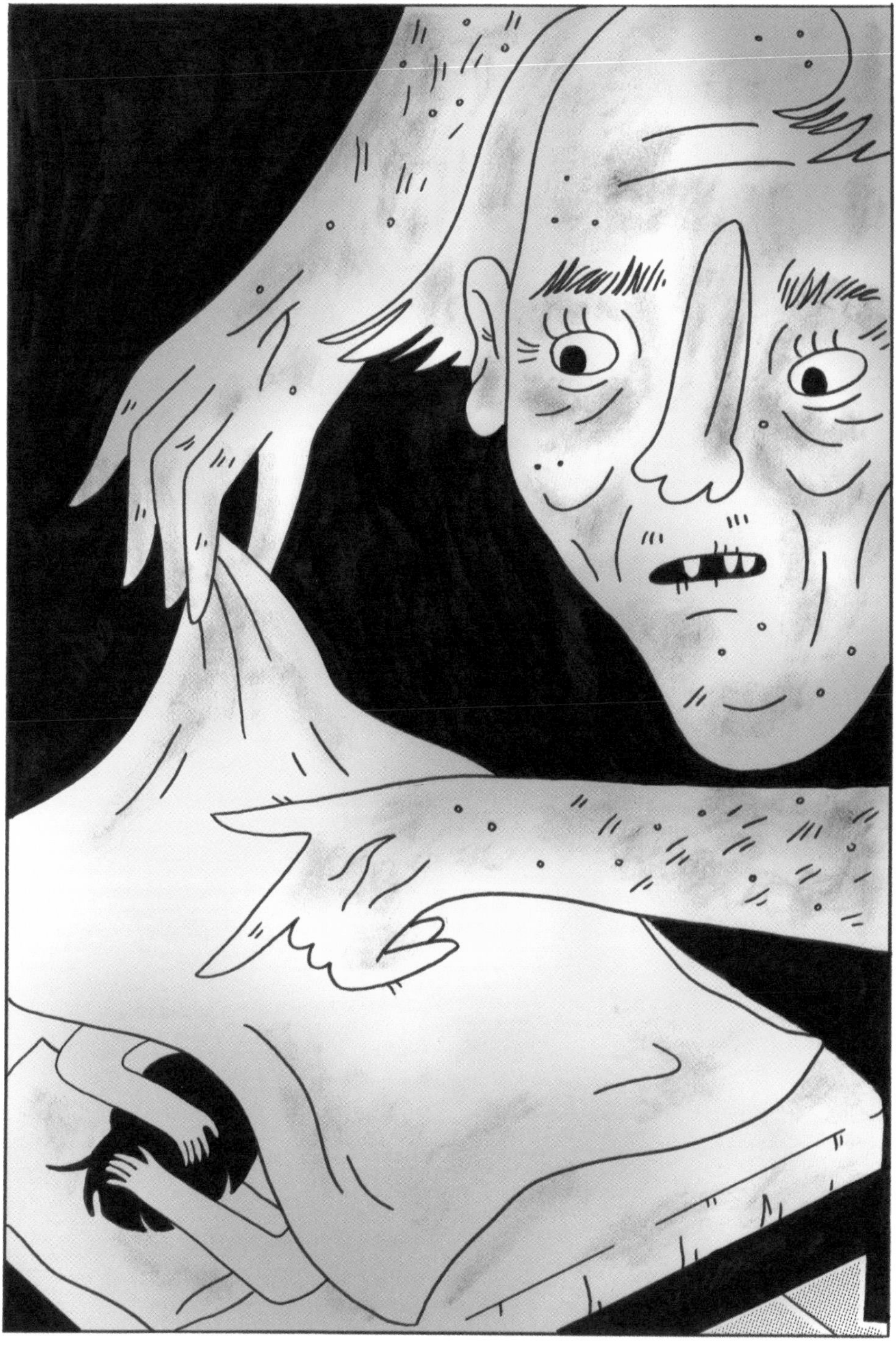

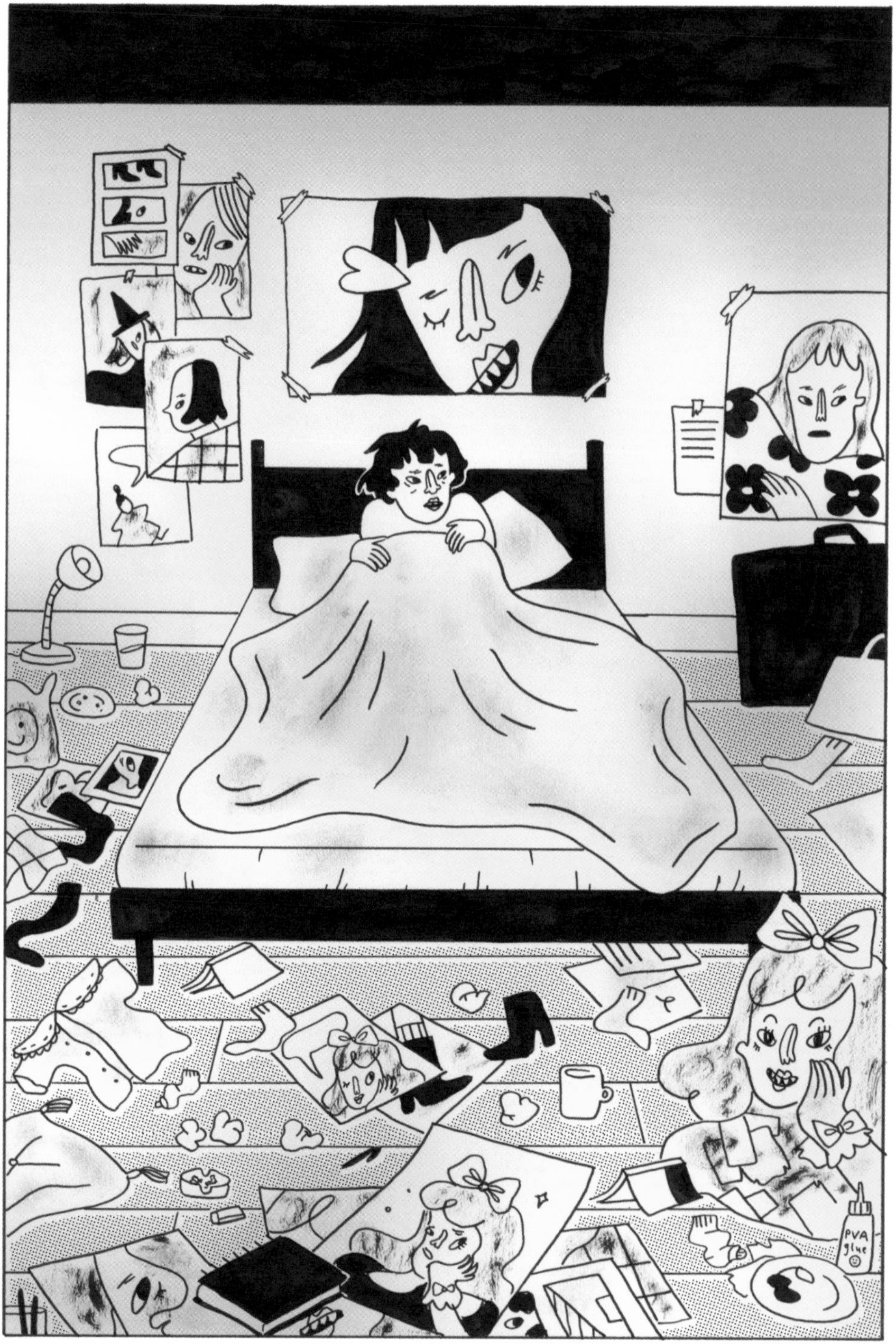
PVA glue

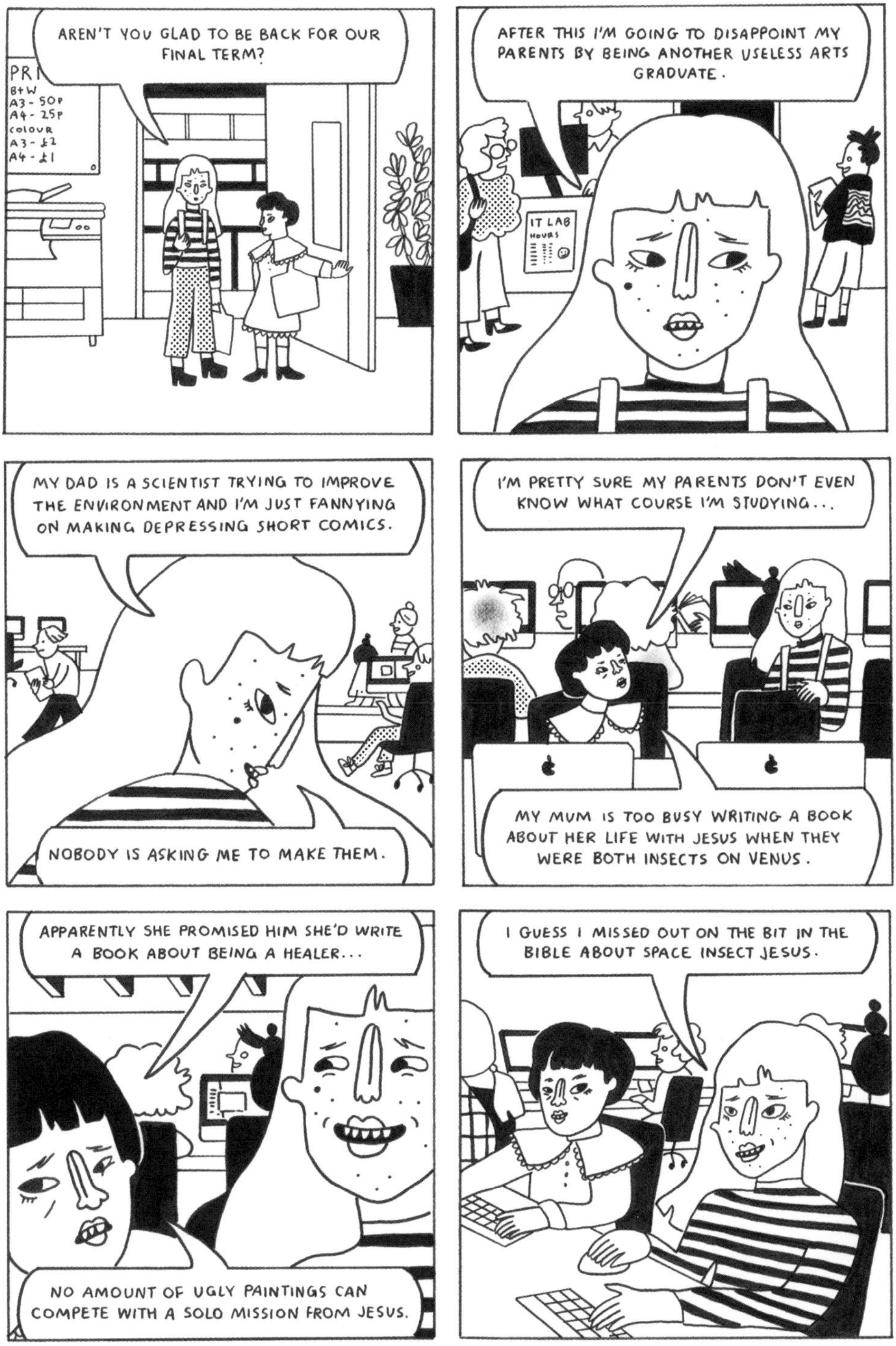
AREN'T YOU GLAD TO BE BACK FOR OUR FINAL TERM?
PRI
B+W
A3 - 50P
A4 - 25P
COLOUR
A3 - £2
A4 - £1
AFTER THIS I'M GOING TO DISAPPOINT MY PARENTS BY BEING ANOTHER USELESS ARTS GRADUATE.
IT LAB
HOURS
MY DAD IS A SCIENTIST TRYING TO IMPROVE THE ENVIRONMENT AND I'M JUST FANNYING ON MAKING DEPRESSING SHORT COMICS.
NOBODY IS ASKING ME TO MAKE THEM.
I'M PRETTY SURE MY PARENTS DON'T EVEN KNOW WHAT COURSE I'M STUDYING...
MY MUM IS TOO BUSY WRITING A BOOK ABOUT HER LIFE WITH JESUS WHEN THEY WERE BOTH INSECTS ON VENUS.
APPARENTLY SHE PROMISED HIM SHE'D WRITE A BOOK ABOUT BEING A HEALER...
NO AMOUNT OF UGLY PAINTINGS CAN COMPETE WITH A SOLO MISSION FROM JESUS.
I GUESS I MISSED OUT ON THE BIT IN THE BIBLE ABOUT SPACE INSECT JESUS.

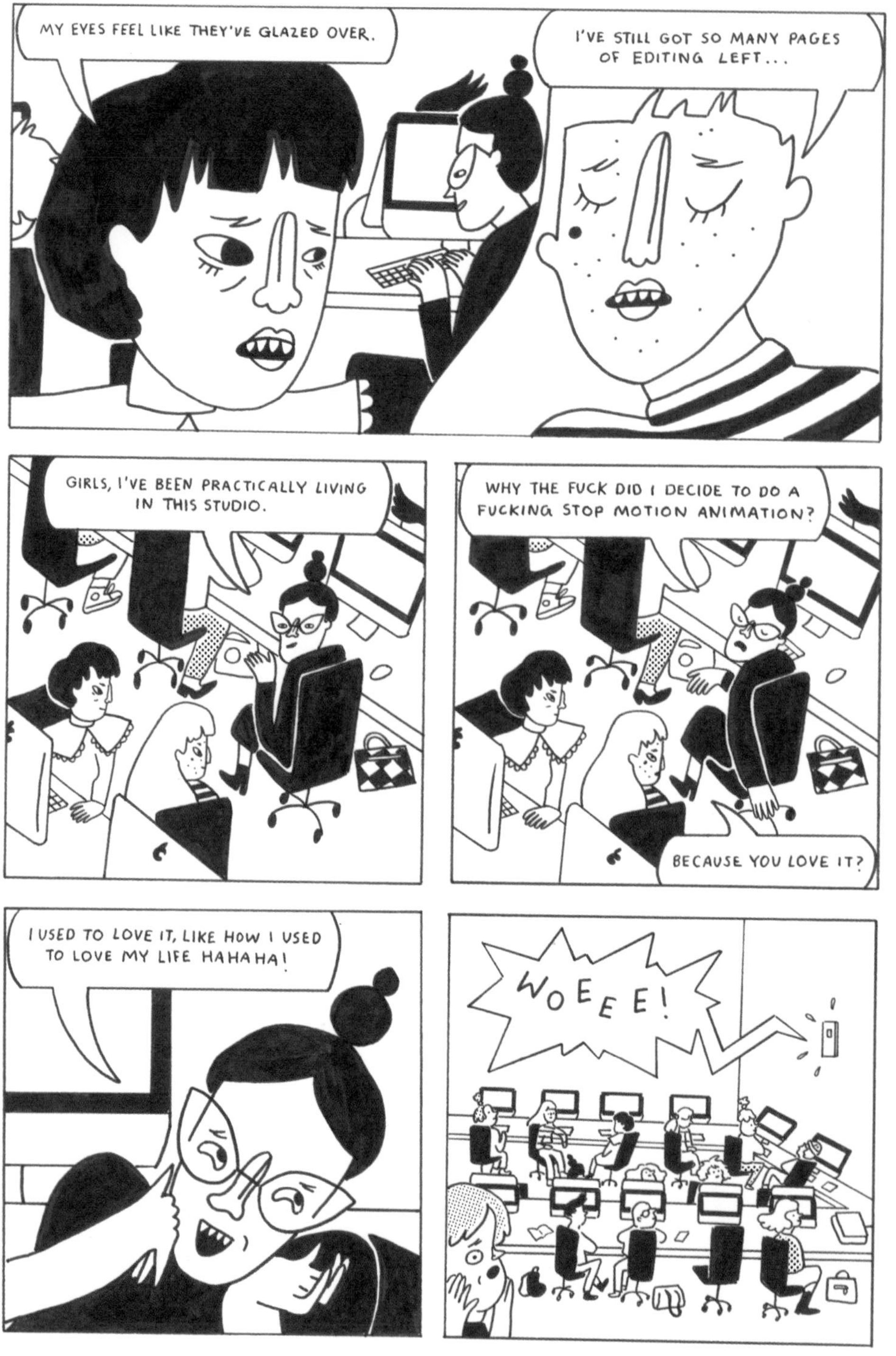
MY EYES FEEL LIKE THEY'VE GLAZED OVER.
I'VE STILL GOT SO MANY PAGES OF EDITING LEFT...
GIRLS, I'VE BEEN PRACTICALLY LIVING IN THIS STUDIO.
WHY THE FUCK DID I DECIDE TO DO A FUCKING STOP MOTION ANIMATION?
BECAUSE YOU LOVE IT?
I USED TO LOVE IT, LIKE HOW I USED TO LOVE MY LIFE HAHAHA!
WOEEE!

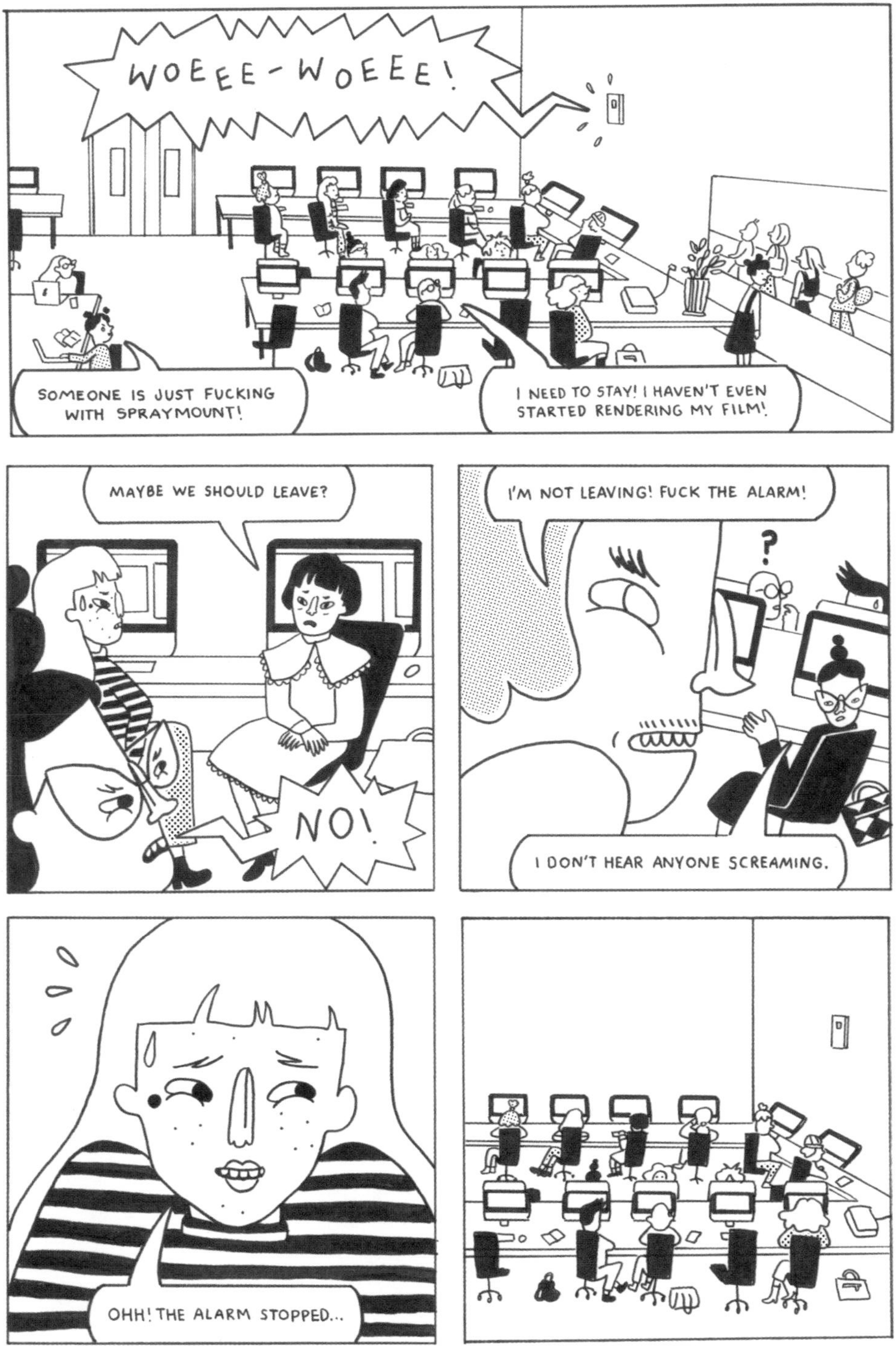
WOEEE-WOEEE!
SOMEONE IS JUST FUCKING WITH SPRAYMOUNT!
I NEED TO STAY! I HAVEN'T EVEN STARTED RENDERING MY FILM!
MAYBE WE SHOULD LEAVE?
NO!
I'M NOT LEAVING! FUCK THE ALARM!
?
I DON'T HEAR ANYONE SCREAMING.
OHH! THE ALARM STOPPED...

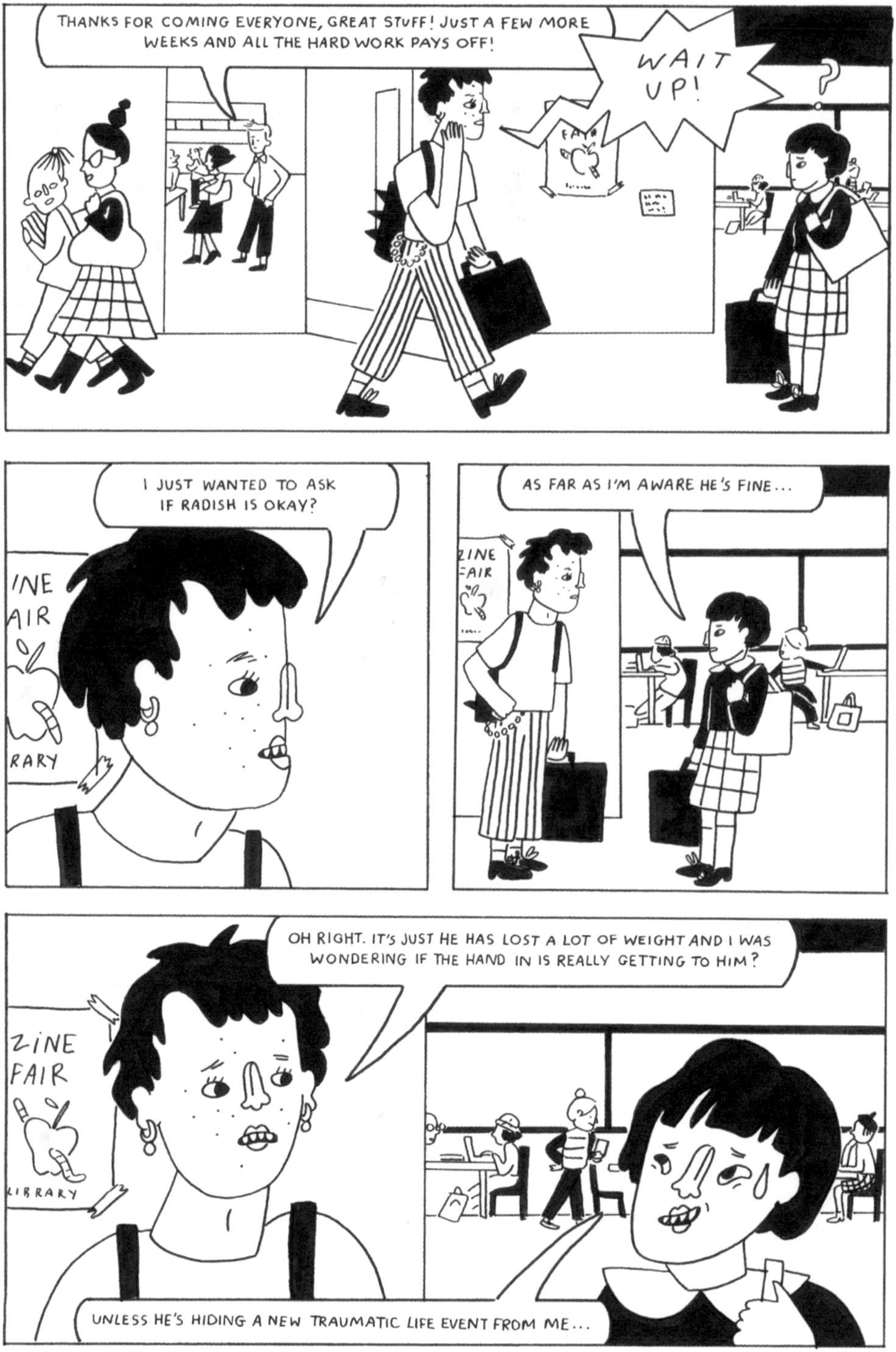
THANKS FOR COMING EVERYONE, GREAT STUFF! JUST A FEW MORE WEEKS AND ALL THE HARD WORK PAYS OFF!
WAIT UP!
?
I JUST WANTED TO ASK IF RADISH IS OKAY?
AS FAR AS I'M AWARE HE'S FINE...
OH RIGHT. IT'S JUST HE HAS LOST A LOT OF WEIGHT AND I WAS WONDERING IF THE HAND IN IS REALLY GETTING TO HIM?
ZINE FAIR
LIBRARY
UNLESS HE'S HIDING A NEW TRAUMATIC LIFE EVENT FROM ME...

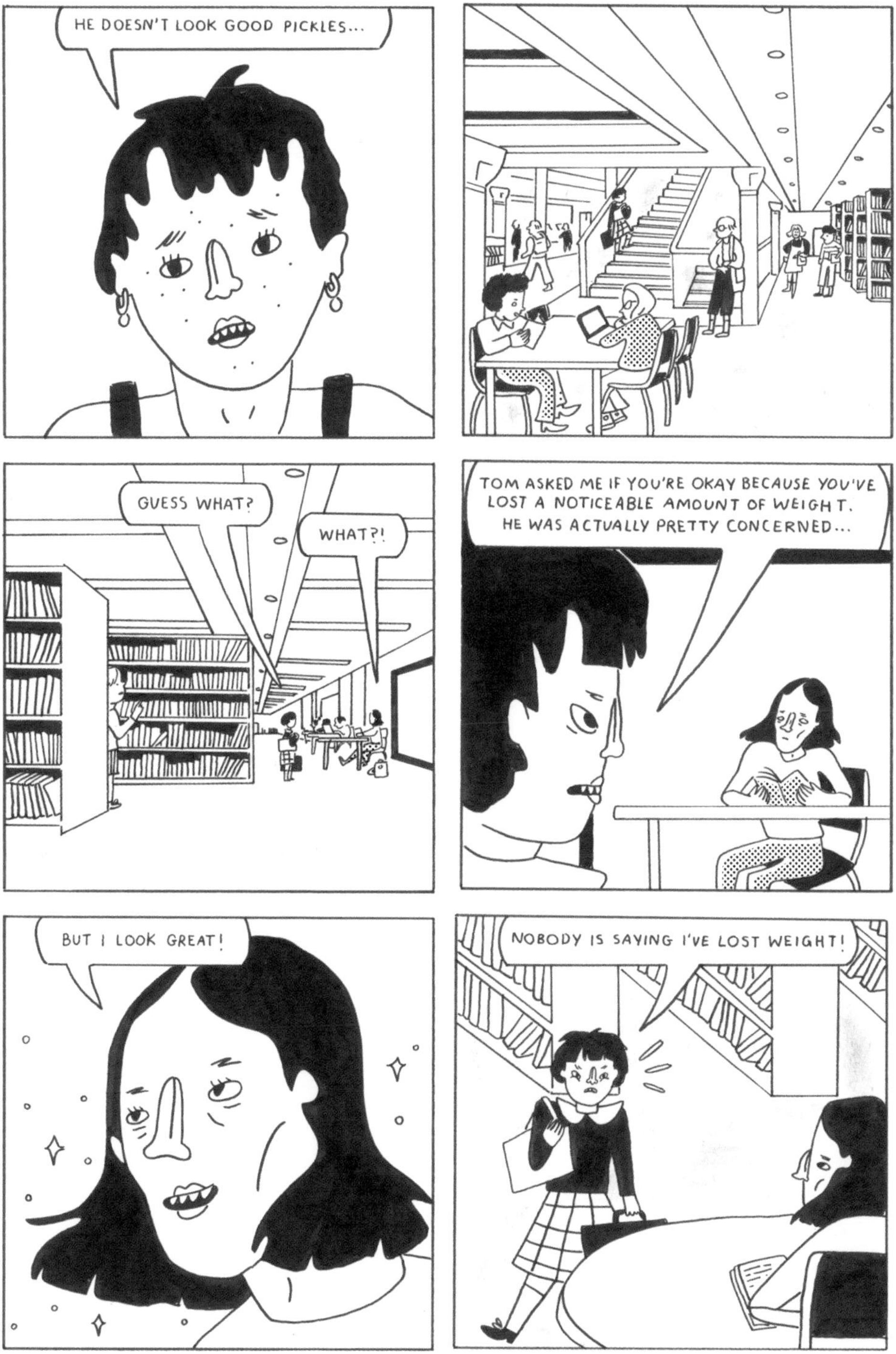
HE DOESN'T LOOK GOOD PICKLES...
GUESS WHAT?
WHAT?!
TOM ASKED ME IF YOU'RE OKAY BECAUSE YOU'VE LOST A NOTICEABLE AMOUNT OF WEIGHT. HE WAS ACTUALLY PRETTY CONCERNED...
BUT I LOOK GREAT!
NOBODY IS SAYING I'VE LOST WEIGHT!

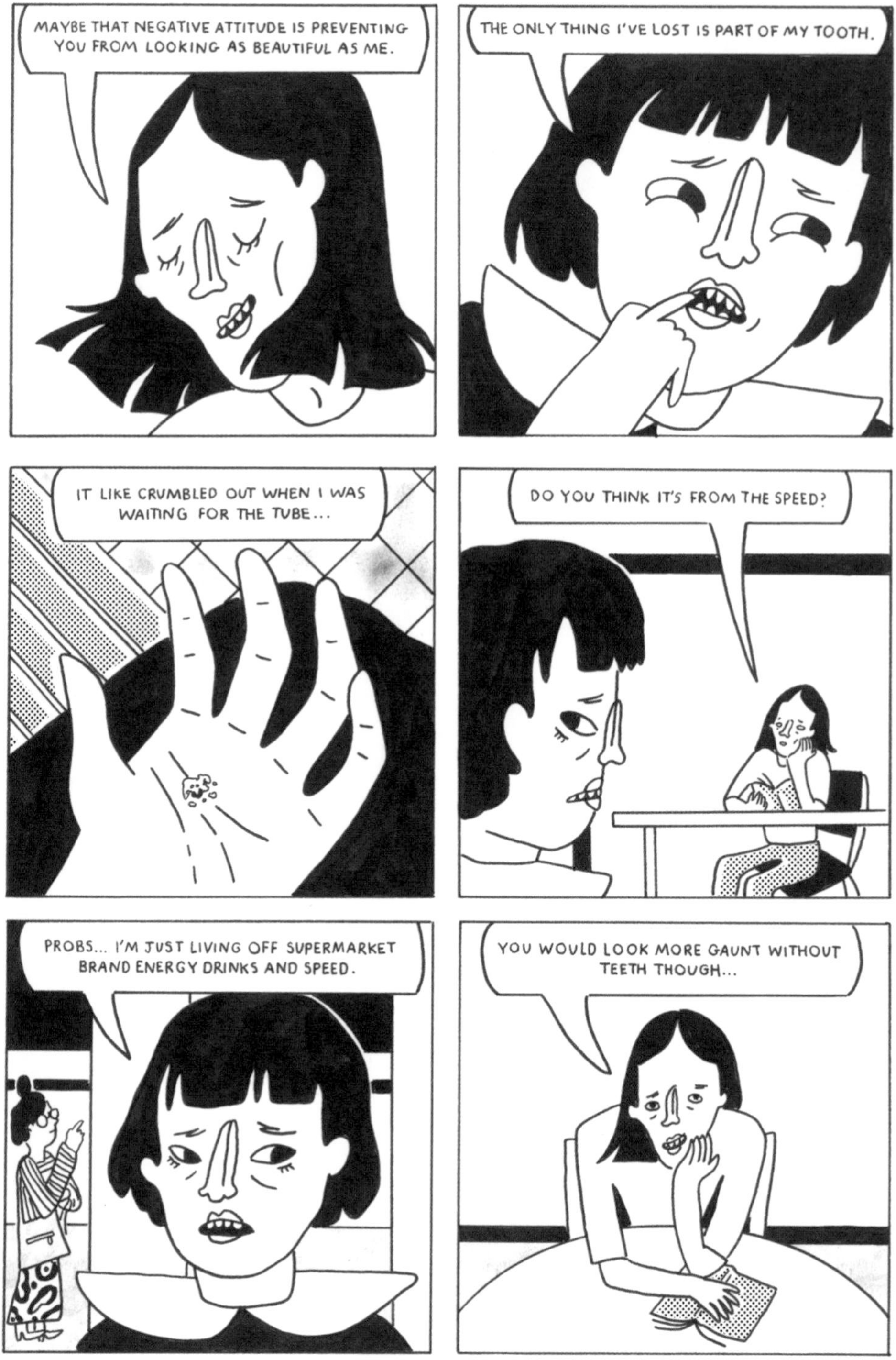
MAYBE THAT NEGATIVE ATTITUDE IS PREVENTING YOU FROM LOOKING AS BEAUTIFUL AS ME.
THE ONLY THING I'VE LOST IS PART OF MY TOOTH.
IT LIKE CRUMBLED OUT WHEN I WAS WAITING FOR THE TUBE...
DO YOU THINK IT'S FROM THE SPEED?
PROBS... I'M JUST LIVING OFF SUPERMARKET BRAND ENERGY DRINKS AND SPEED.
YOU WOULD LOOK MORE GAUNT WITHOUT TEETH THOUGH...

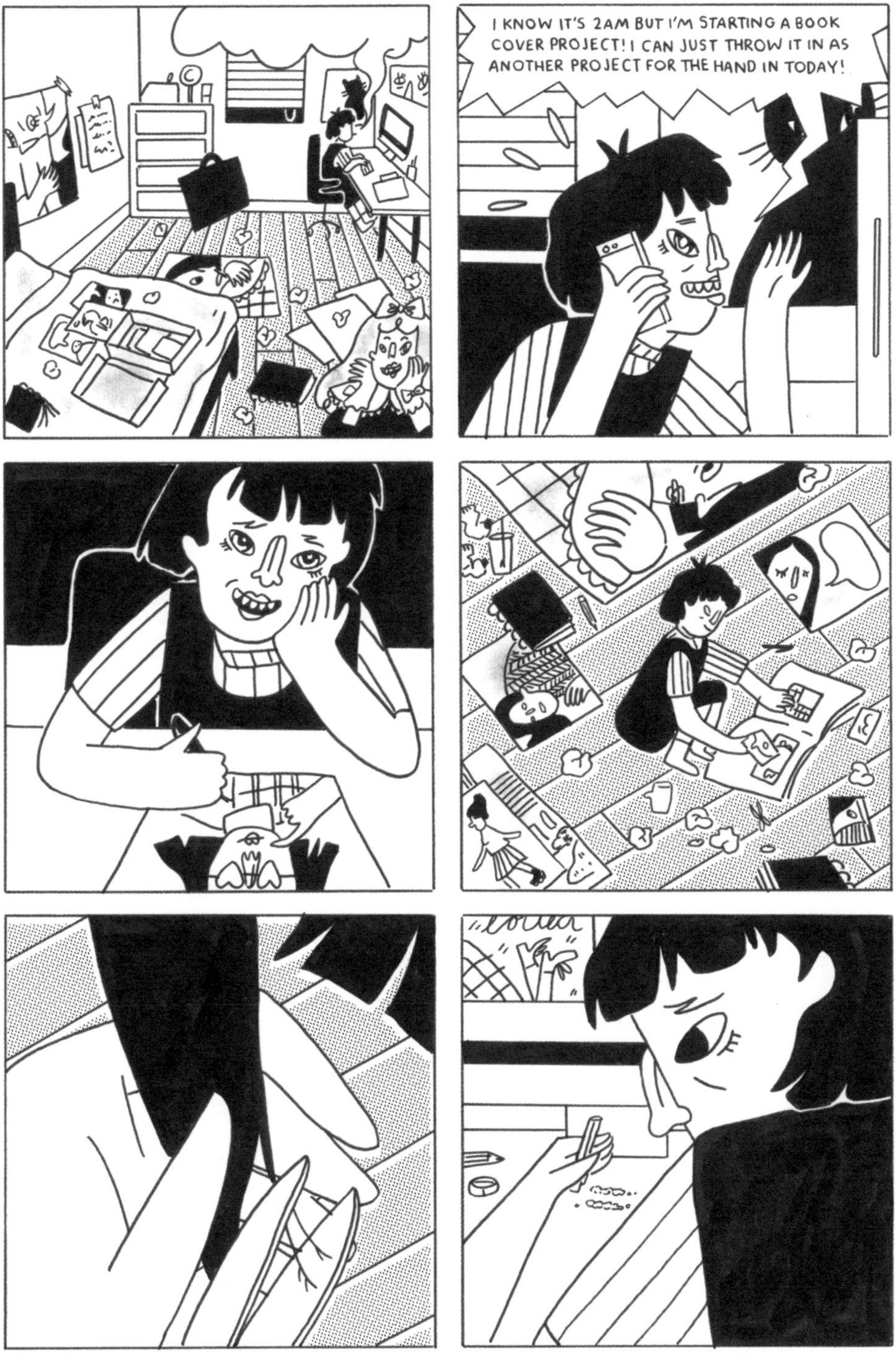
I KNOW IT'S 2AM BUT I'M STARTING A BOOK COVER PROJECT! I CAN JUST THROW IT IN AS ANOTHER PROJECT FOR THE HAND IN TODAY!

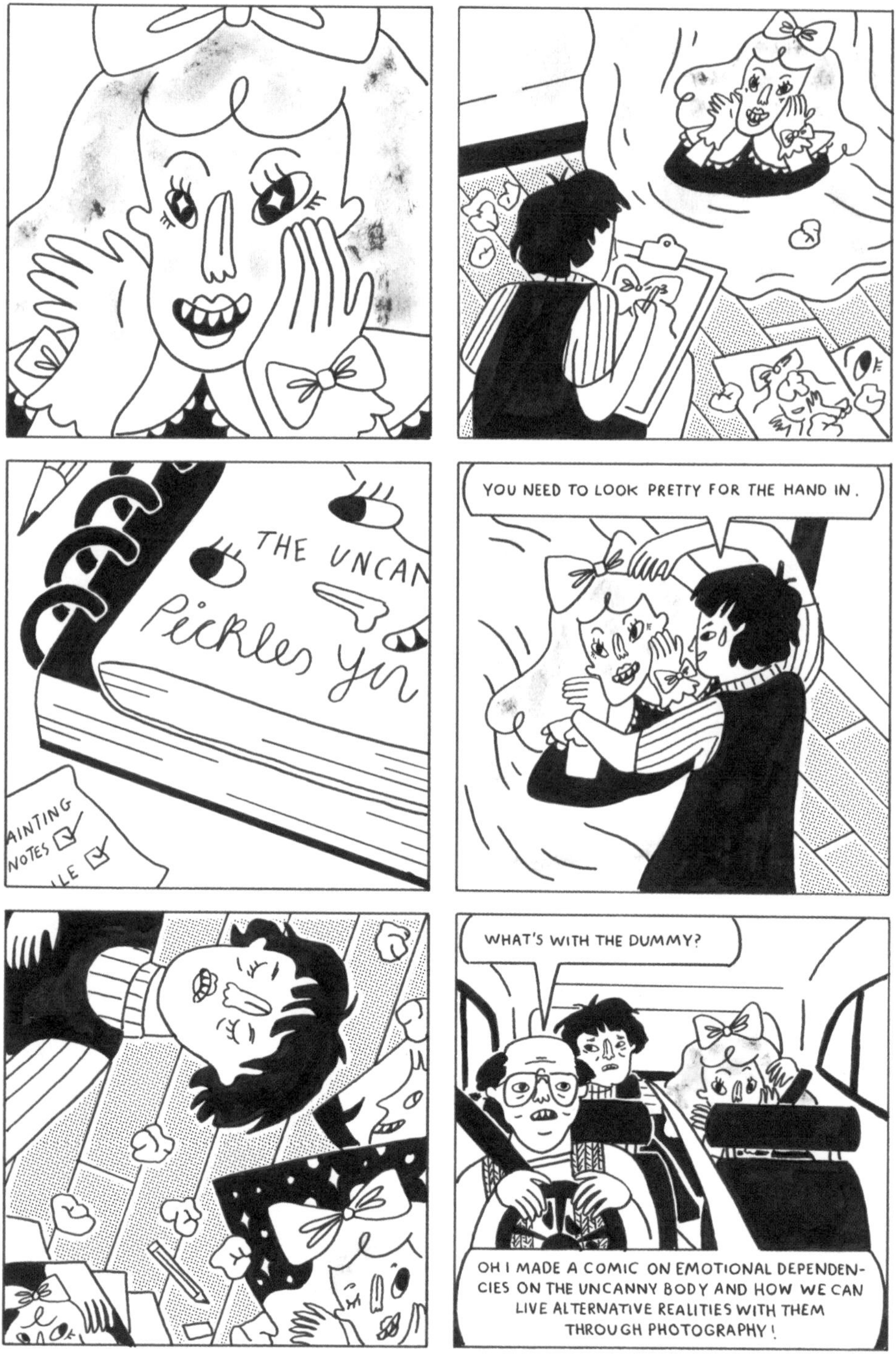
THE UNCAN
Pickles Yu
AINTING
NOTES
YOU NEED TO LOOK PRETTY FOR THE HAND IN.
WHAT'S WITH THE DUMMY?
OH I MADE A COMIC ON EMOTIONAL DEPENDENCIES ON THE UNCANNY BODY AND HOW WE CAN LIVE ALTERNATIVE REALITIES WITH THEM THROUGH PHOTOGRAPHY!

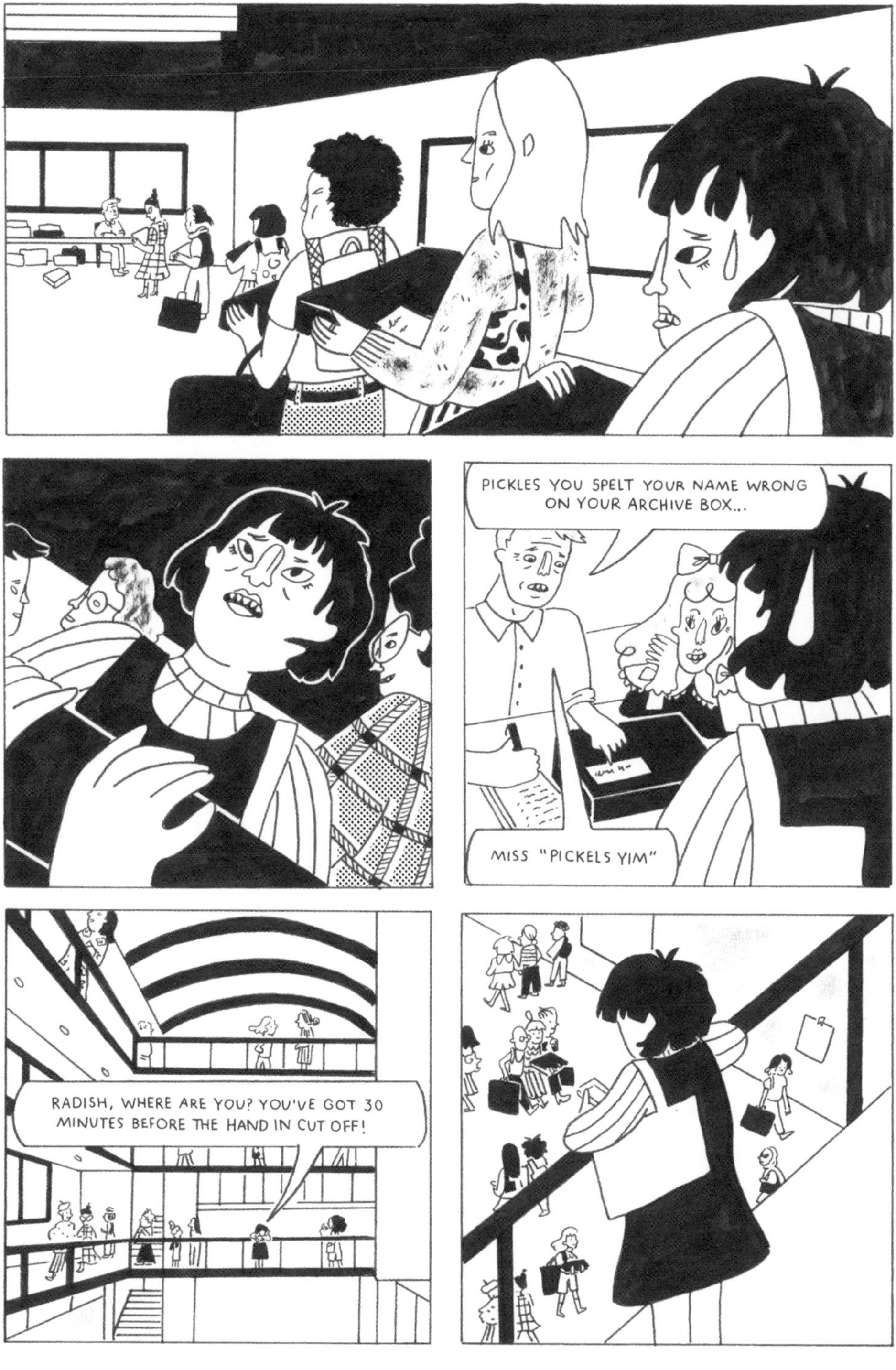
PICKLES YOU SPELT YOUR NAME WRONG ON YOUR ARCHIVE BOX...
MISS "PICKELS YIM"
RADISH, WHERE ARE YOU? YOU'VE GOT 30 MINUTES BEFORE THE HAND IN CUT OFF!

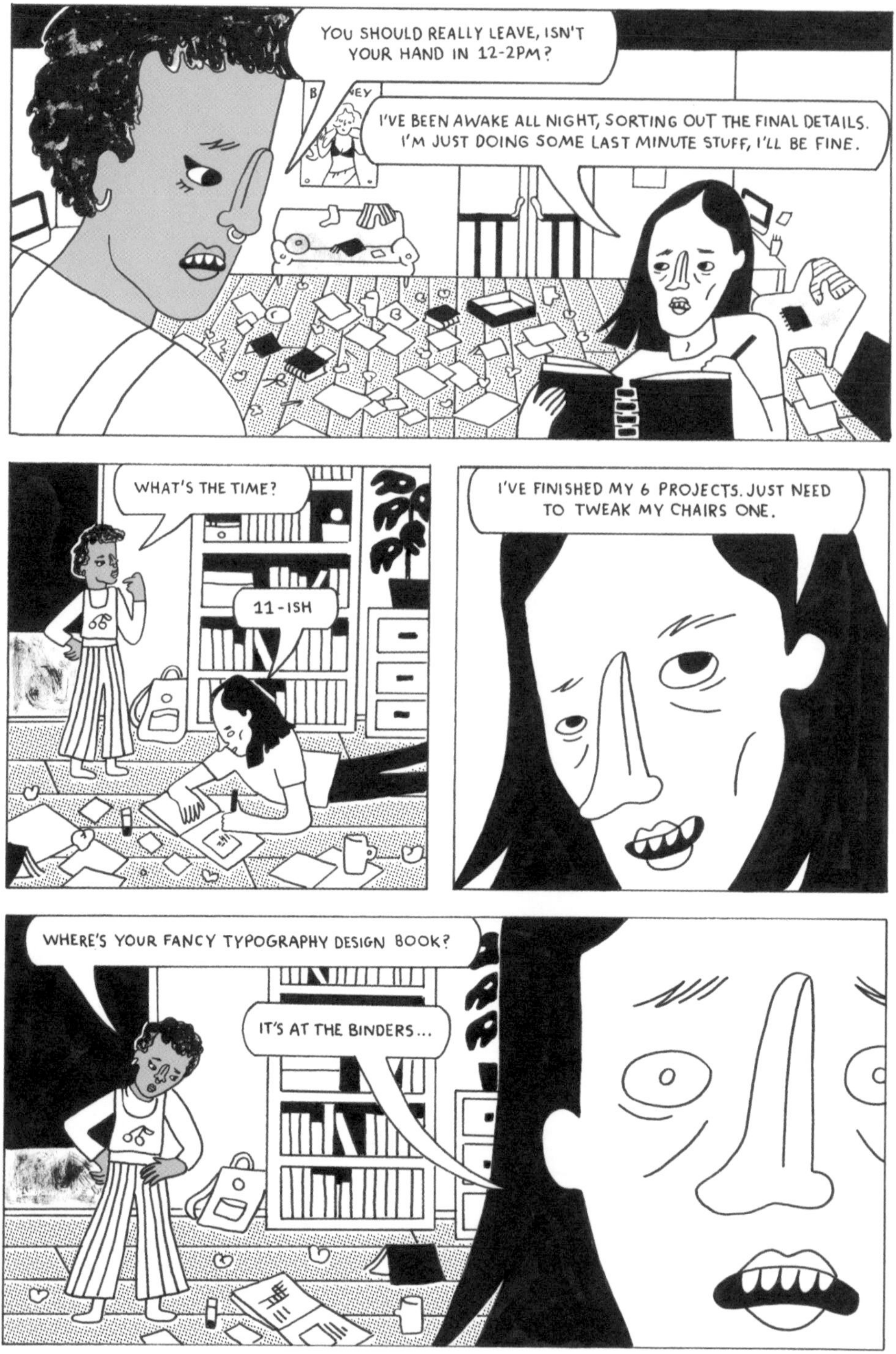
YOU SHOULD REALLY LEAVE, ISN'T YOUR HAND IN 12-2PM?
I'VE BEEN AWAKE ALL NIGHT, SORTING OUT THE FINAL DETAILS. I'M JUST DOING SOME LAST MINUTE STUFF, I'LL BE FINE.
WHAT'S THE TIME?
11-ISH
I'VE FINISHED MY 6 PROJECTS. JUST NEED TO TWEAK MY CHAIRS ONE.
WHERE'S YOUR FANCY TYPOGRAPHY DESIGN BOOK?
IT'S AT THE BINDERS...

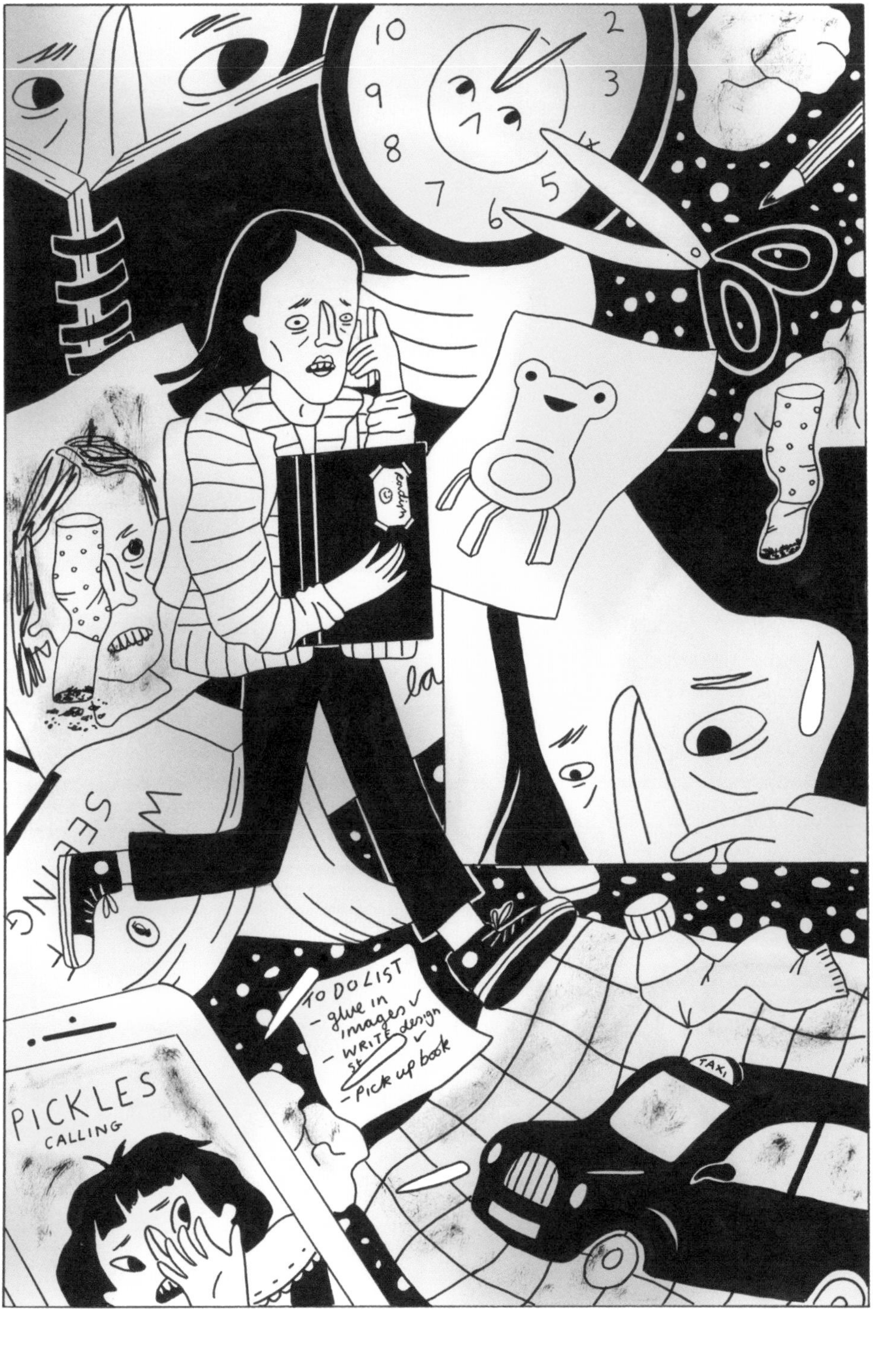
TO DO LIST
- glue in images ✓
- WRITE design st ✓
- Pick up book
PICKLES
CALLING
TAXI
SEEING

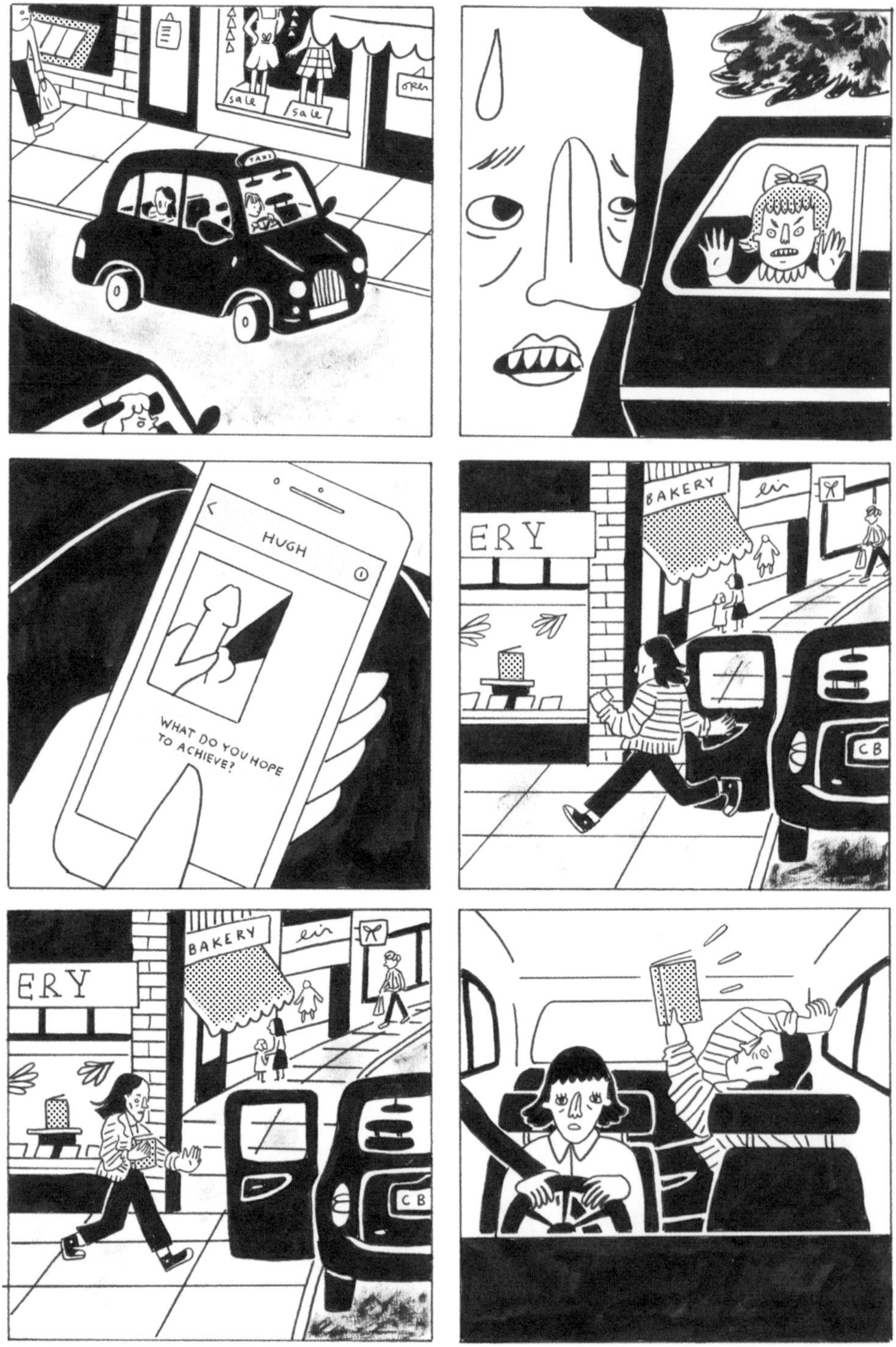
sale
sale
open
TAXI
HUGH
WHAT DO YOU HOPE TO ACHIEVE?
ERY
BAKERY
CB
ERY
BAKERY
CB

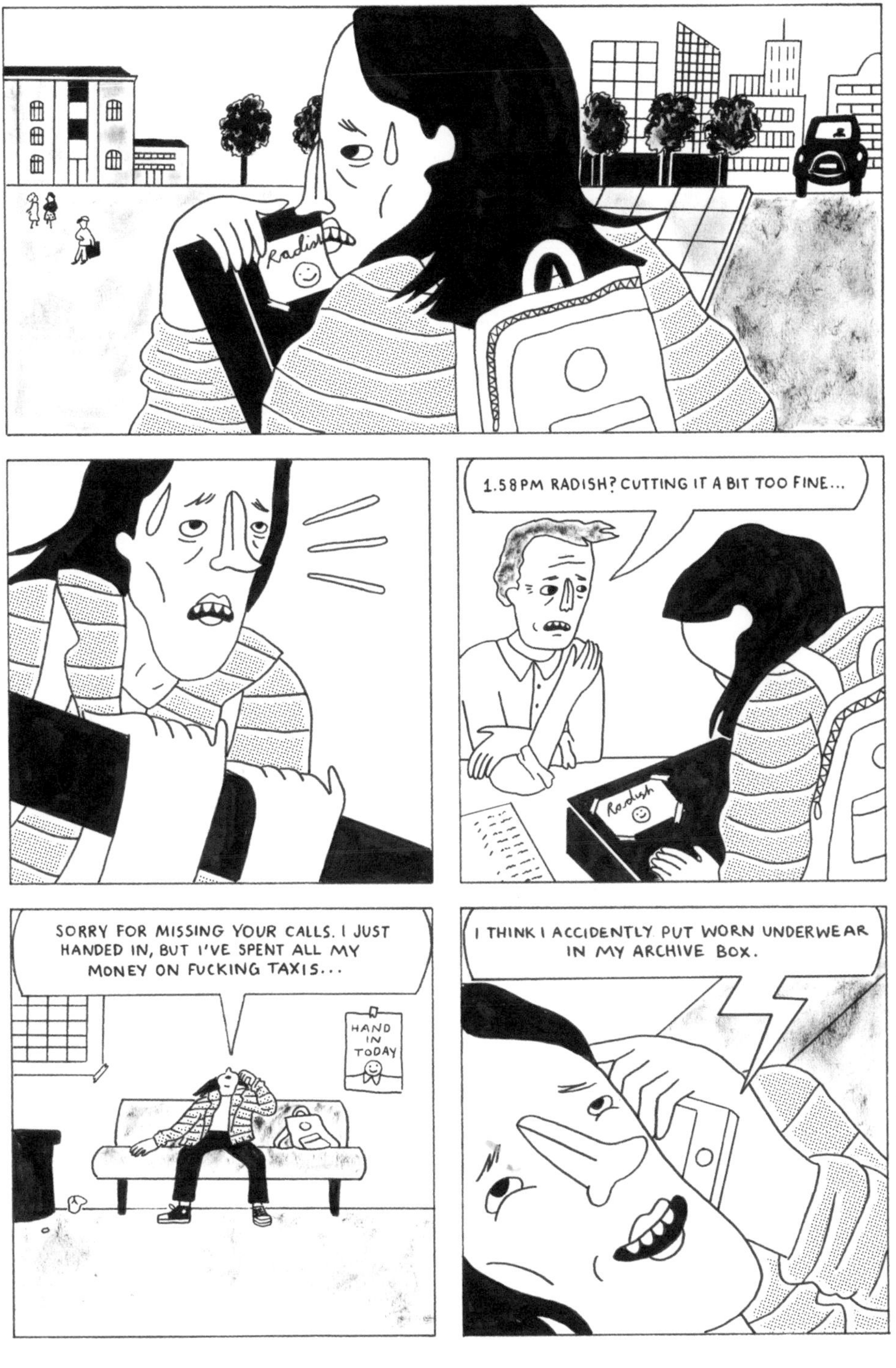
Radish
1.58PM RADISH? CUTTING IT A BIT TOO FINE...
Radish
SORRY FOR MISSING YOUR CALLS. I JUST HANDED IN, BUT I'VE SPENT ALL MY MONEY ON FUCKING TAXIS...
HAND IN TODAY
I THINK I ACCIDENTLY PUT WORN UNDERWEAR IN MY ARCHIVE BOX.

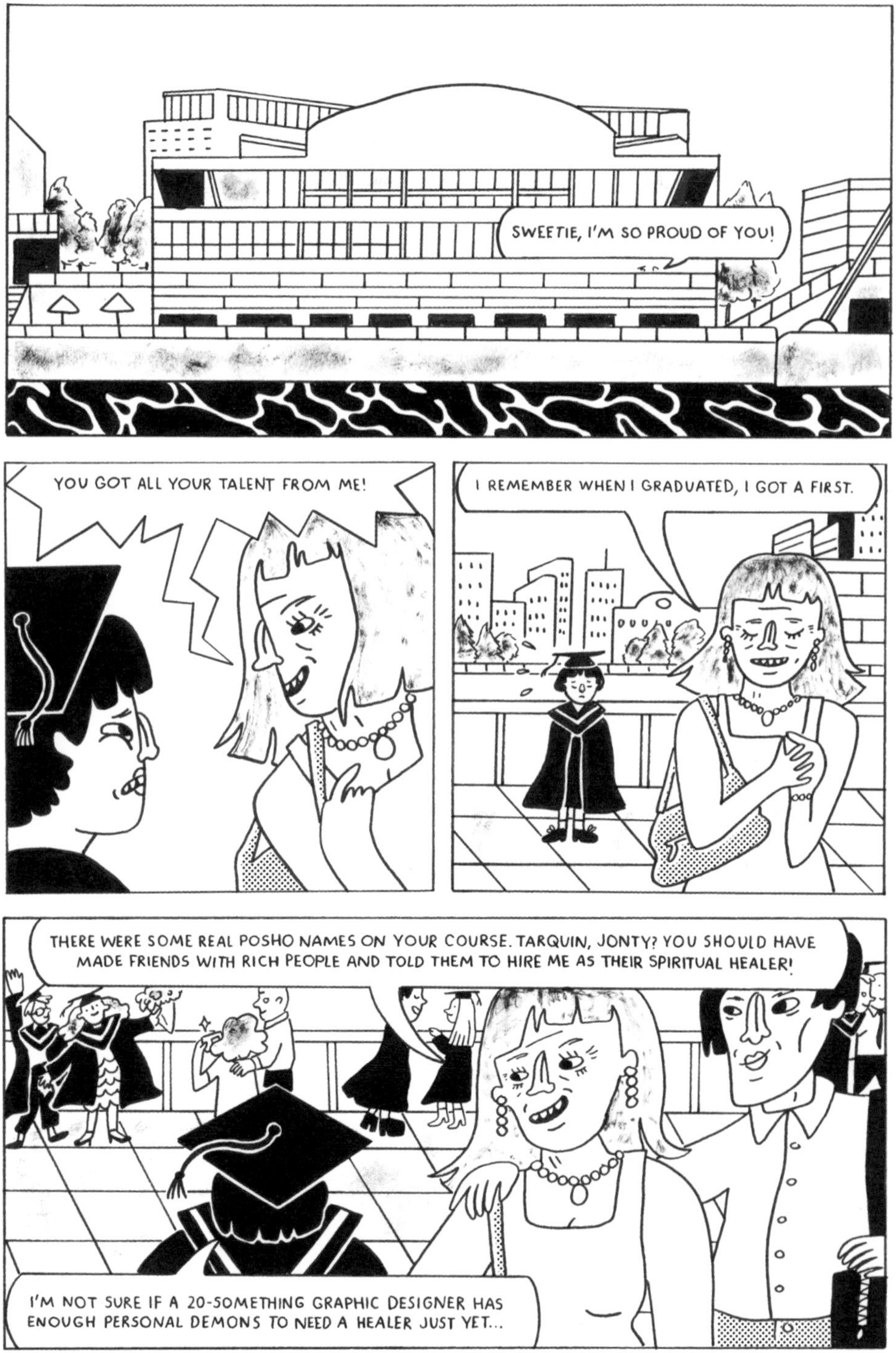
SWEETIE, I'M SO PROUD OF YOU!
YOU GOT ALL YOUR TALENT FROM ME!
I REMEMBER WHEN I GRADUATED, I GOT A FIRST.
THERE WERE SOME REAL POSHO NAMES ON YOUR COURSE. TARQUIN, JONTY? YOU SHOULD HAVE MADE FRIENDS WITH RICH PEOPLE AND TOLD THEM TO HIRE ME AS THEIR SPIRITUAL HEALER!
I'M NOT SURE IF A 20-SOMETHING GRAPHIC DESIGNER HAS ENOUGH PERSONAL DEMONS TO NEED A HEALER JUST YET...

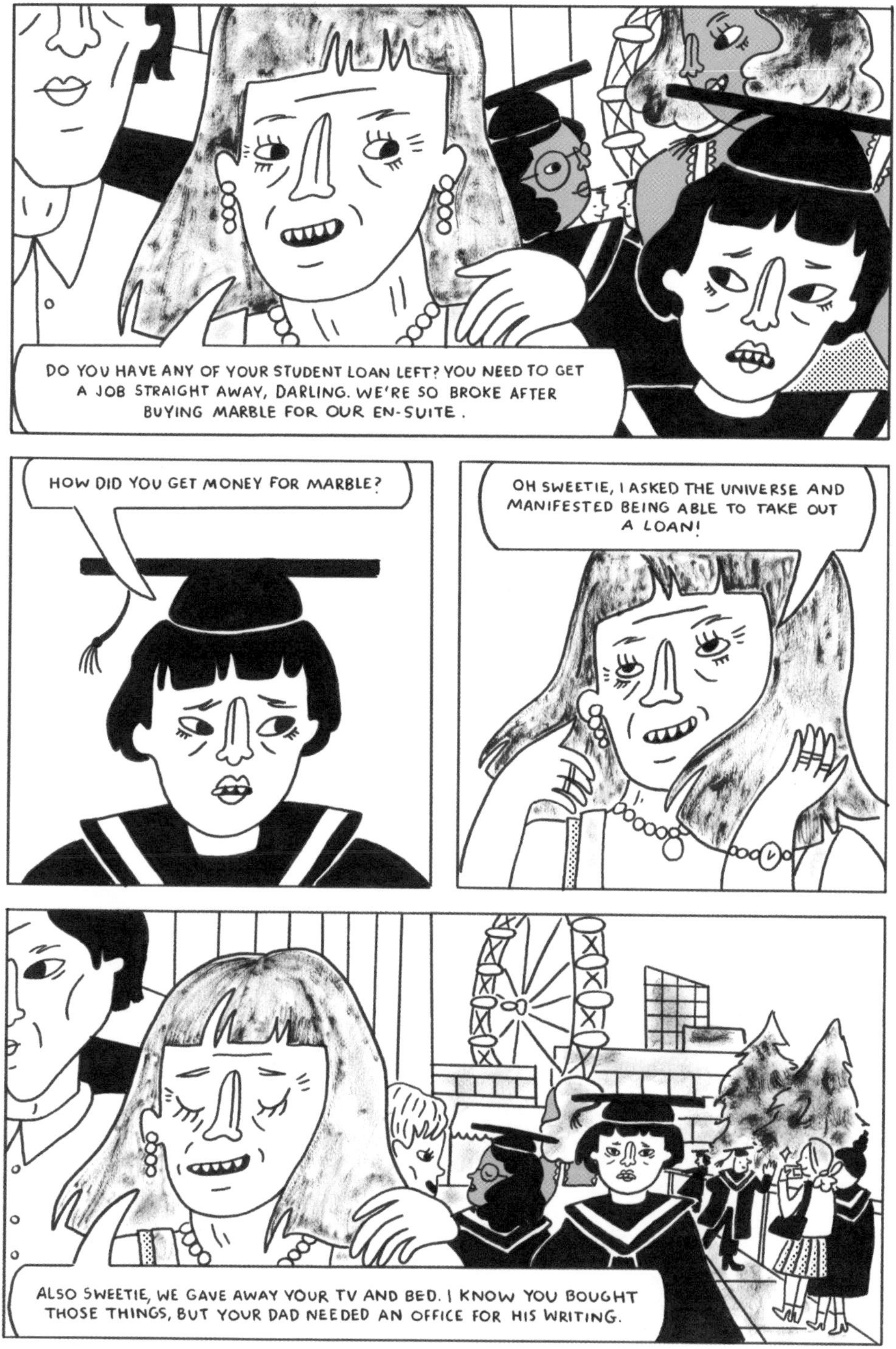
DO YOU HAVE ANY OF YOUR STUDENT LOAN LEFT? YOU NEED TO GET A JOB STRAIGHT AWAY, DARLING. WE'RE SO BROKE AFTER BUYING MARBLE FOR OUR EN-SUITE.
HOW DID YOU GET MONEY FOR MARBLE?
OH SWEETIE, I ASKED THE UNIVERSE AND MANIFESTED BEING ABLE TO TAKE OUT A LOAN!
ALSO SWEETIE, WE GAVE AWAY YOUR TV AND BED. I KNOW YOU BOUGHT THOSE THINGS, BUT YOUR DAD NEEDED AN OFFICE FOR HIS WRITING.

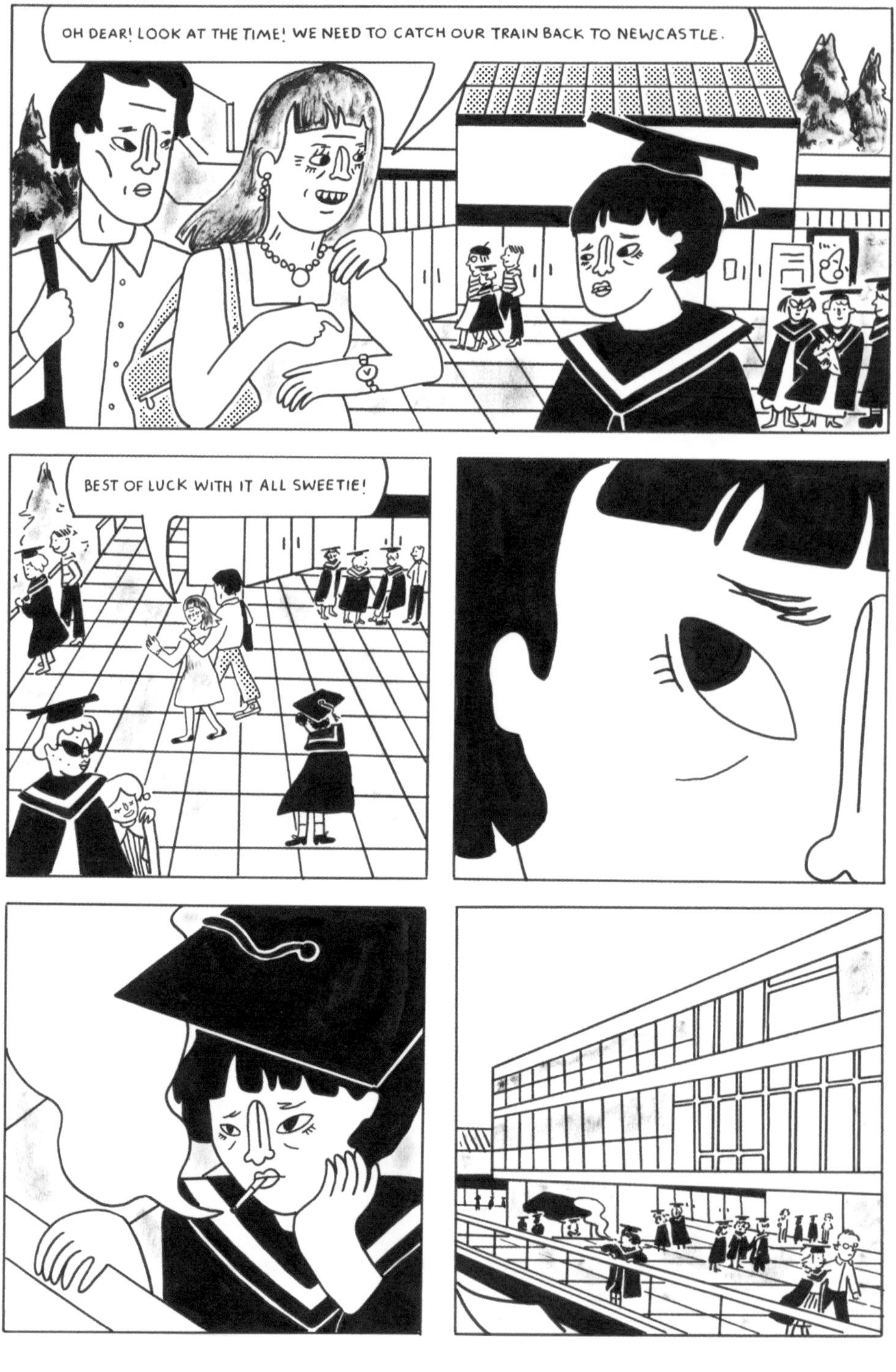
OH DEAR! LOOK AT THE TIME! WE NEED TO CATCH OUR TRAIN BACK TO NEWCASTLE.
BEST OF LUCK WITH IT ALL SWEETIE!

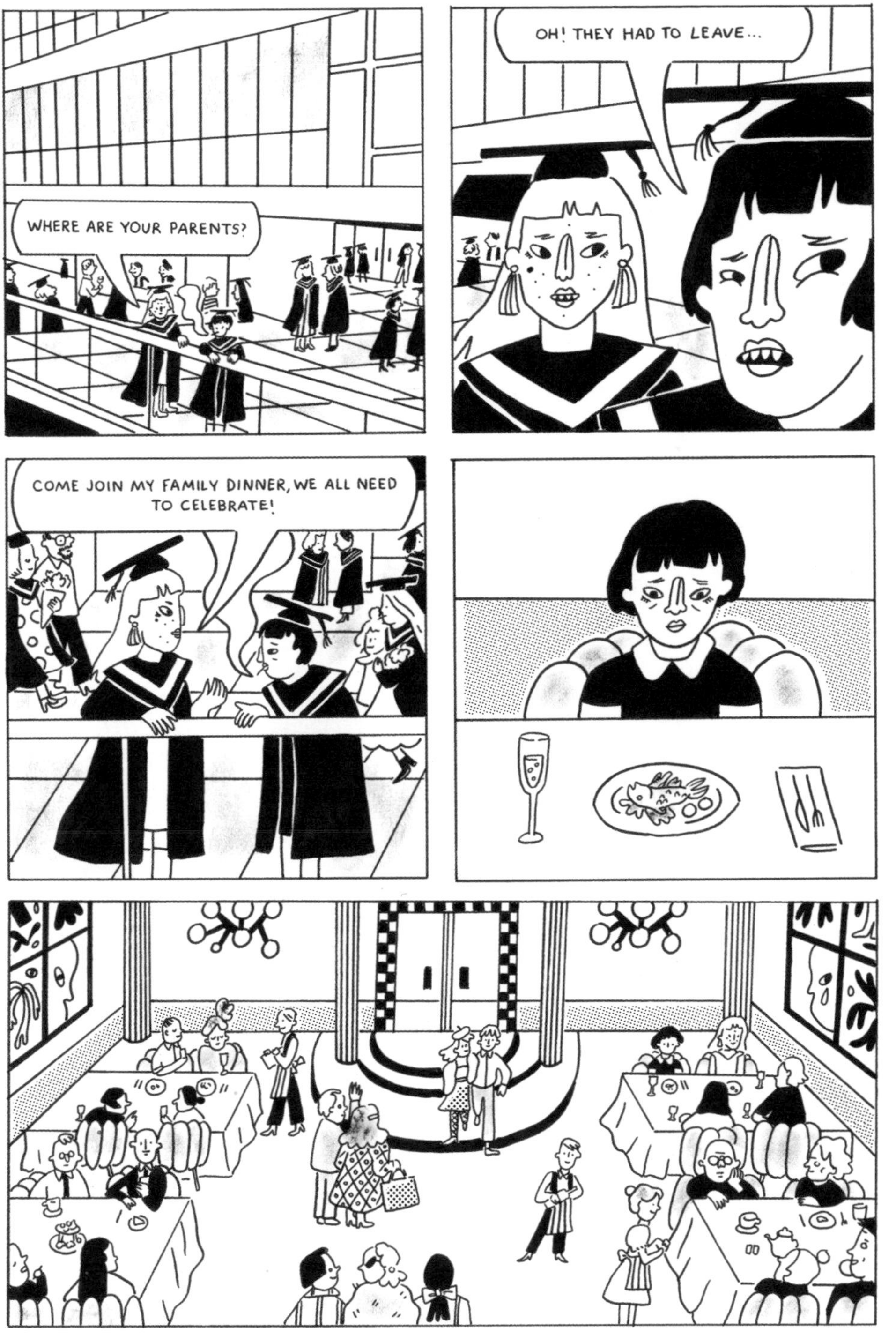
WHERE ARE YOUR PARENTS?
OH! THEY HAD TO LEAVE...
COME JOIN MY FAMILY DINNER, WE ALL NEED TO CELEBRATE!

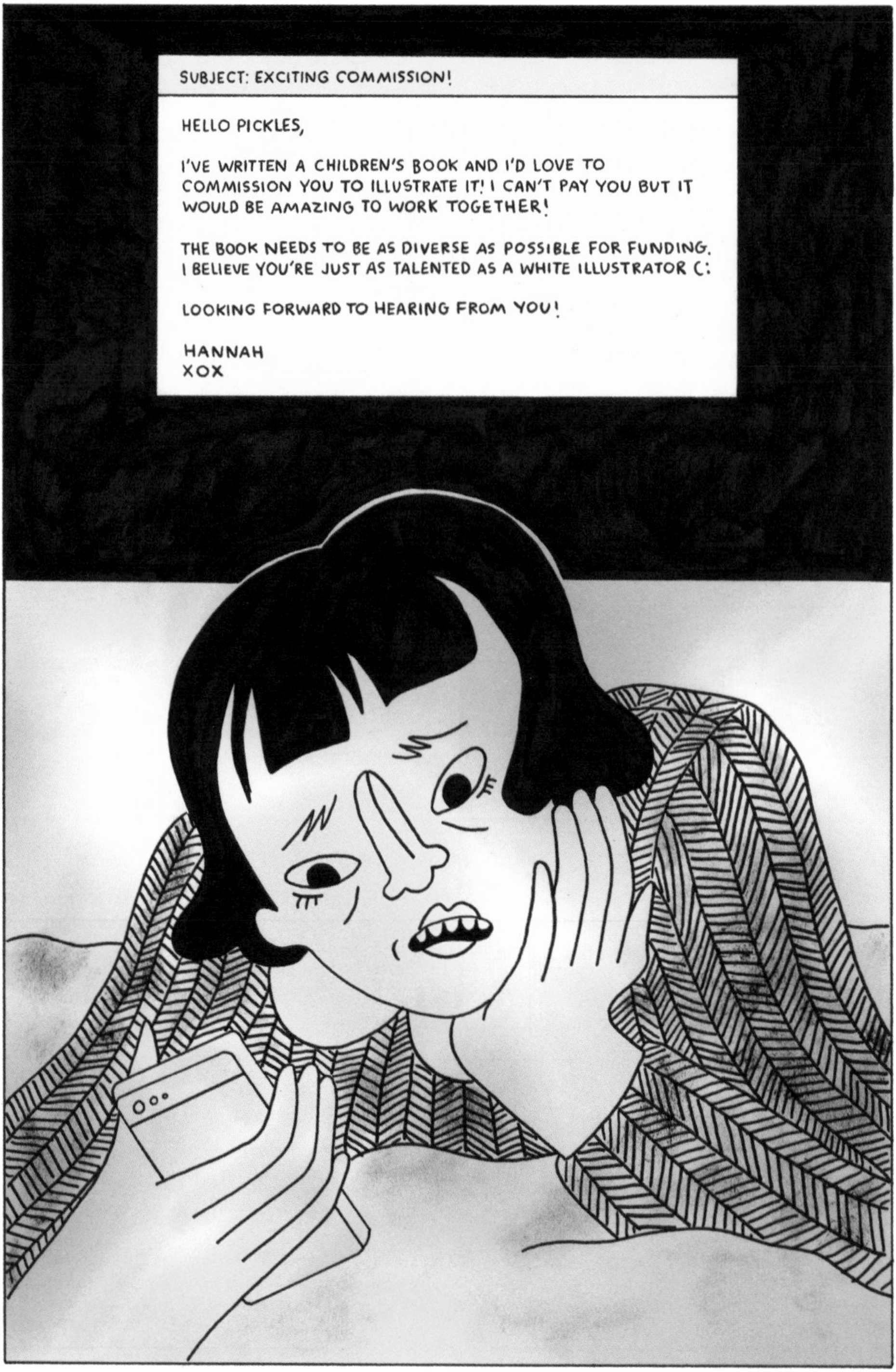
SUBJECT: EXCITING COMMISSION!
HELLO PICKLES,
I'VE WRITTEN A CHILDREN'S BOOK AND I'D LOVE TO COMMISSION YOU TO ILLUSTRATE IT! I CAN'T PAY YOU BUT IT WOULD BE AMAZING TO WORK TOGETHER!
THE BOOK NEEDS TO BE AS DIVERSE AS POSSIBLE FOR FUNDING. I BELIEVE YOU'RE JUST AS TALENTED AS A WHITE ILLUSTRATOR (:
LOOKING FORWARD TO HEARING FROM YOU!
HANNAH
XOX

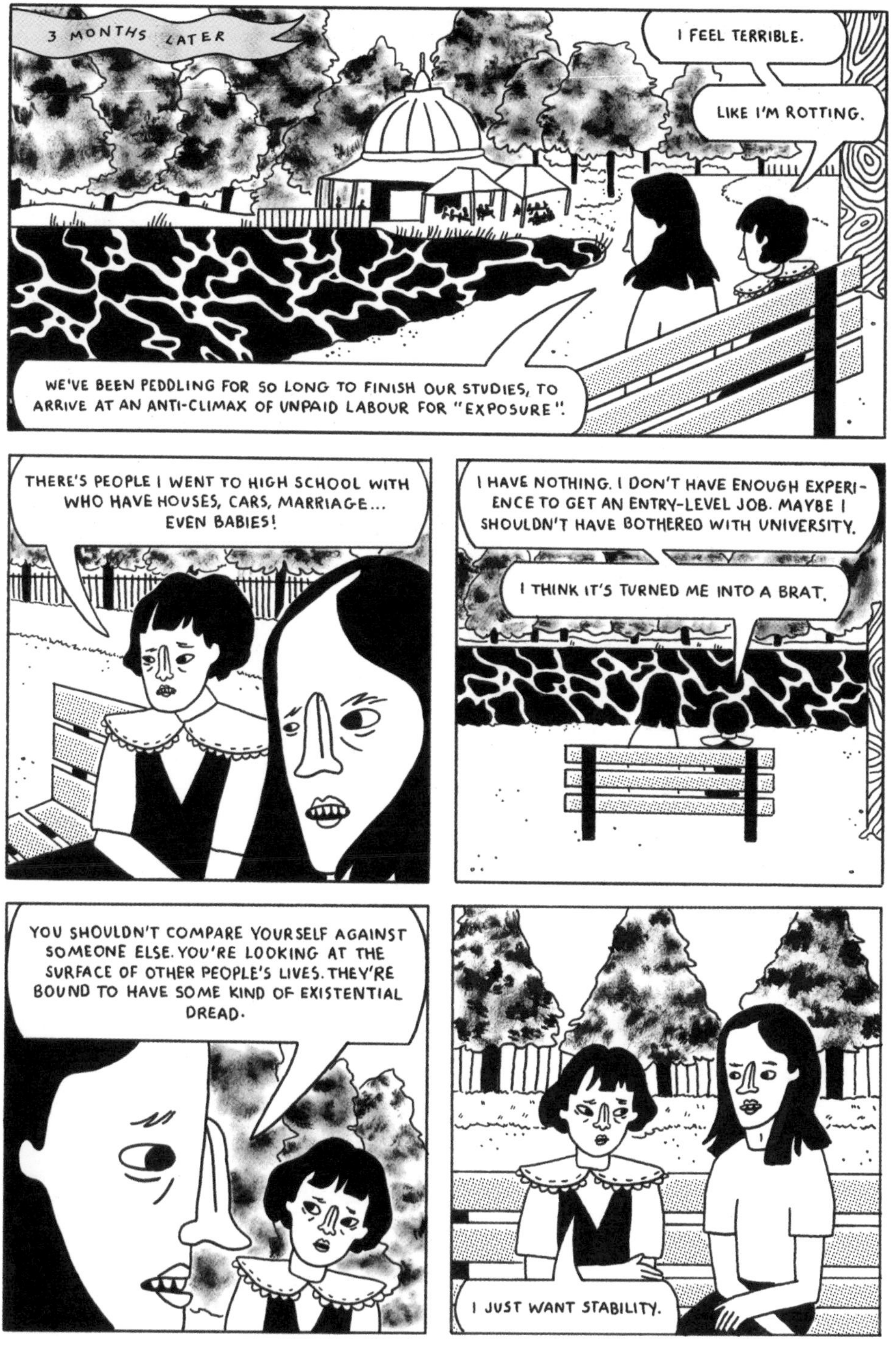
3 MONTHS LATER
I FEEL TERRIBLE.
LIKE I'M ROTTING.
WE'VE BEEN PEDDLING FOR SO LONG TO FINISH OUR STUDIES, TO ARRIVE AT AN ANTI-CLIMAX OF UNPAID LABOUR FOR "EXPOSURE".
THERE'S PEOPLE I WENT TO HIGH SCHOOL WITH WHO HAVE HOUSES, CARS, MARRIAGE... EVEN BABIES!
I HAVE NOTHING. I DON'T HAVE ENOUGH EXPERIENCE TO GET AN ENTRY-LEVEL JOB. MAYBE I SHOULDN'T HAVE BOTHERED WITH UNIVERSITY.
I THINK IT'S TURNED ME INTO A BRAT.
YOU SHOULDN'T COMPARE YOURSELF AGAINST SOMEONE ELSE. YOU'RE LOOKING AT THE SURFACE OF OTHER PEOPLE'S LIVES. THEY'RE BOUND TO HAVE SOME KIND OF EXISTENTIAL DREAD.
I JUST WANT STABILITY.

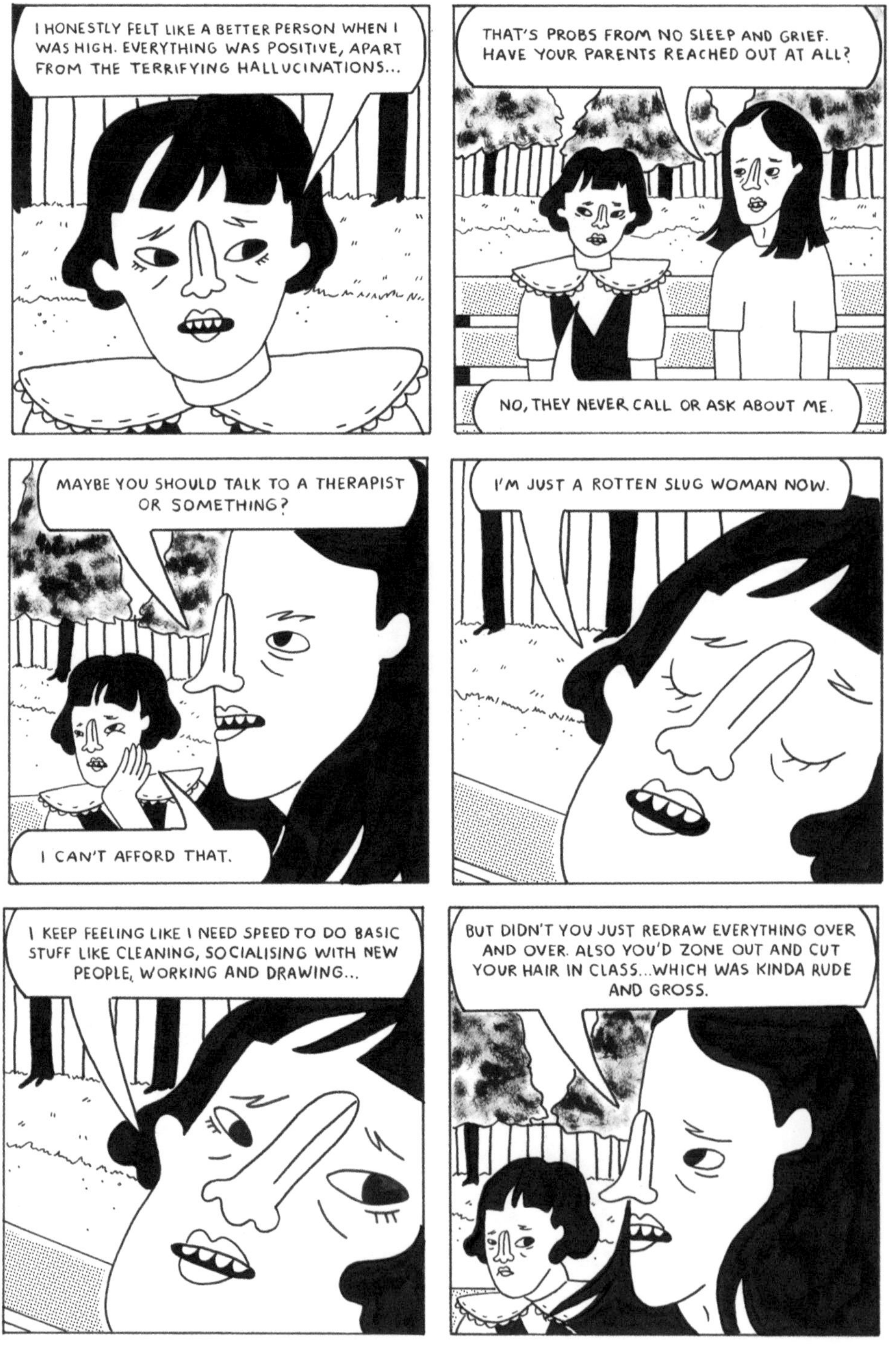

I HONESTLY FELT LIKE A BETTER PERSON WHEN I WAS HIGH. EVERYTHING WAS POSITIVE, APART FROM THE TERRIFYING HALLUCINATIONS...
THAT'S PROBS FROM NO SLEEP AND GRIEF. HAVE YOUR PARENTS REACHED OUT AT ALL?
NO, THEY NEVER CALL OR ASK ABOUT ME.
MAYBE YOU SHOULD TALK TO A THERAPIST OR SOMETHING?
I CAN'T AFFORD THAT.
I'M JUST A ROTTEN SLUG WOMAN NOW.
I KEEP FEELING LIKE I NEED SPEED TO DO BASIC STUFF LIKE CLEANING, SOCIALISING WITH NEW PEOPLE, WORKING AND DRAWING...
BUT DIDN'T YOU JUST REDRAW EVERYTHING OVER AND OVER. ALSO YOU'D ZONE OUT AND CUT YOUR HAIR IN CLASS...WHICH WAS KINDA RUDE AND GROSS.

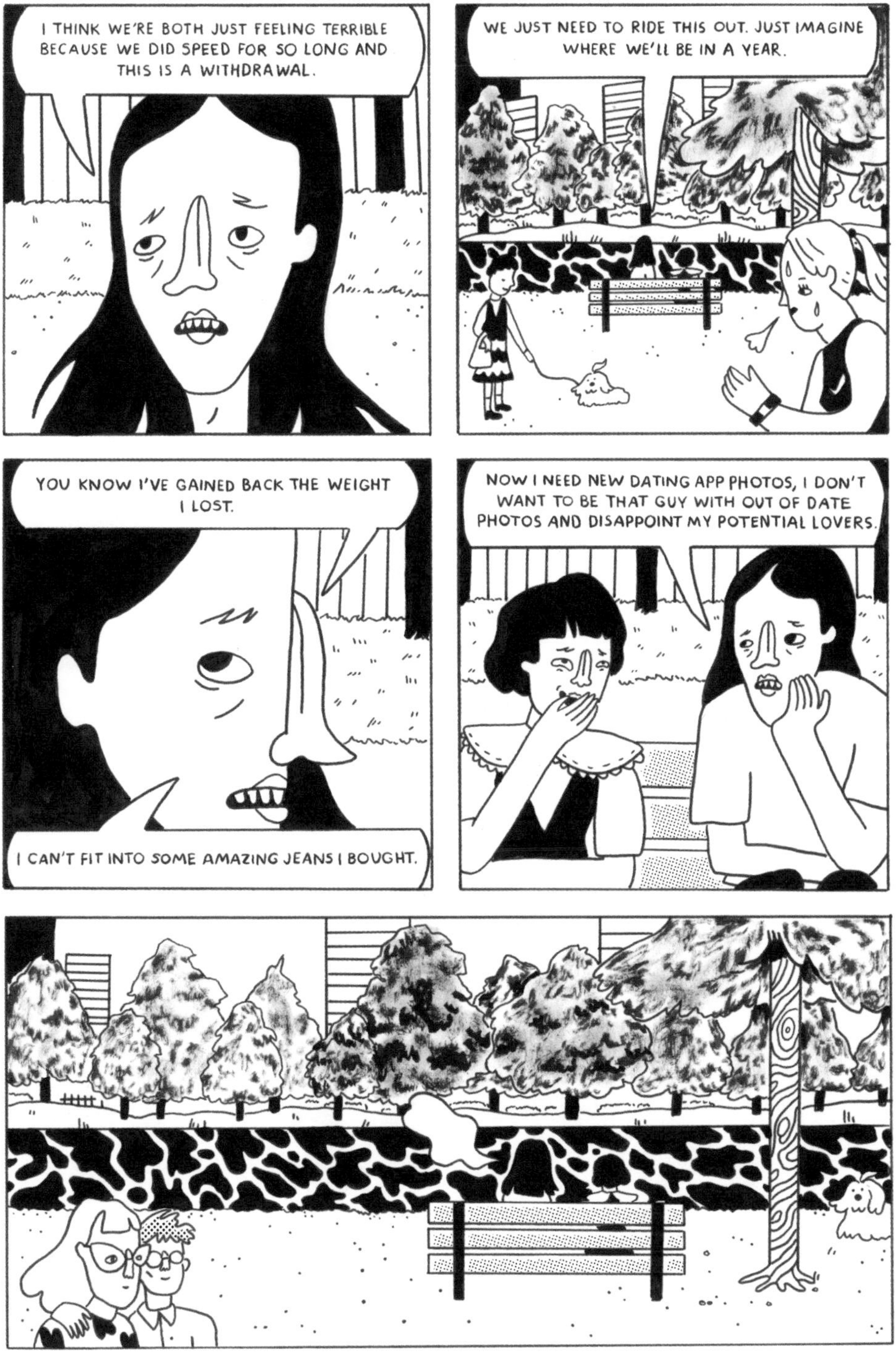
I THINK WE'RE BOTH JUST FEELING TERRIBLE BECAUSE WE DID SPEED FOR SO LONG AND THIS IS A WITHDRAWAL.
WE JUST NEED TO RIDE THIS OUT. JUST IMAGINE WHERE WE'LL BE IN A YEAR.
YOU KNOW I'VE GAINED BACK THE WEIGHT I LOST.
I CAN'T FIT INTO SOME AMAZING JEANS I BOUGHT.
NOW I NEED NEW DATING APP PHOTOS, I DON'T WANT TO BE THAT GUY WITH OUT OF DATE PHOTOS AND DISAPPOINT MY POTENTIAL LOVERS.

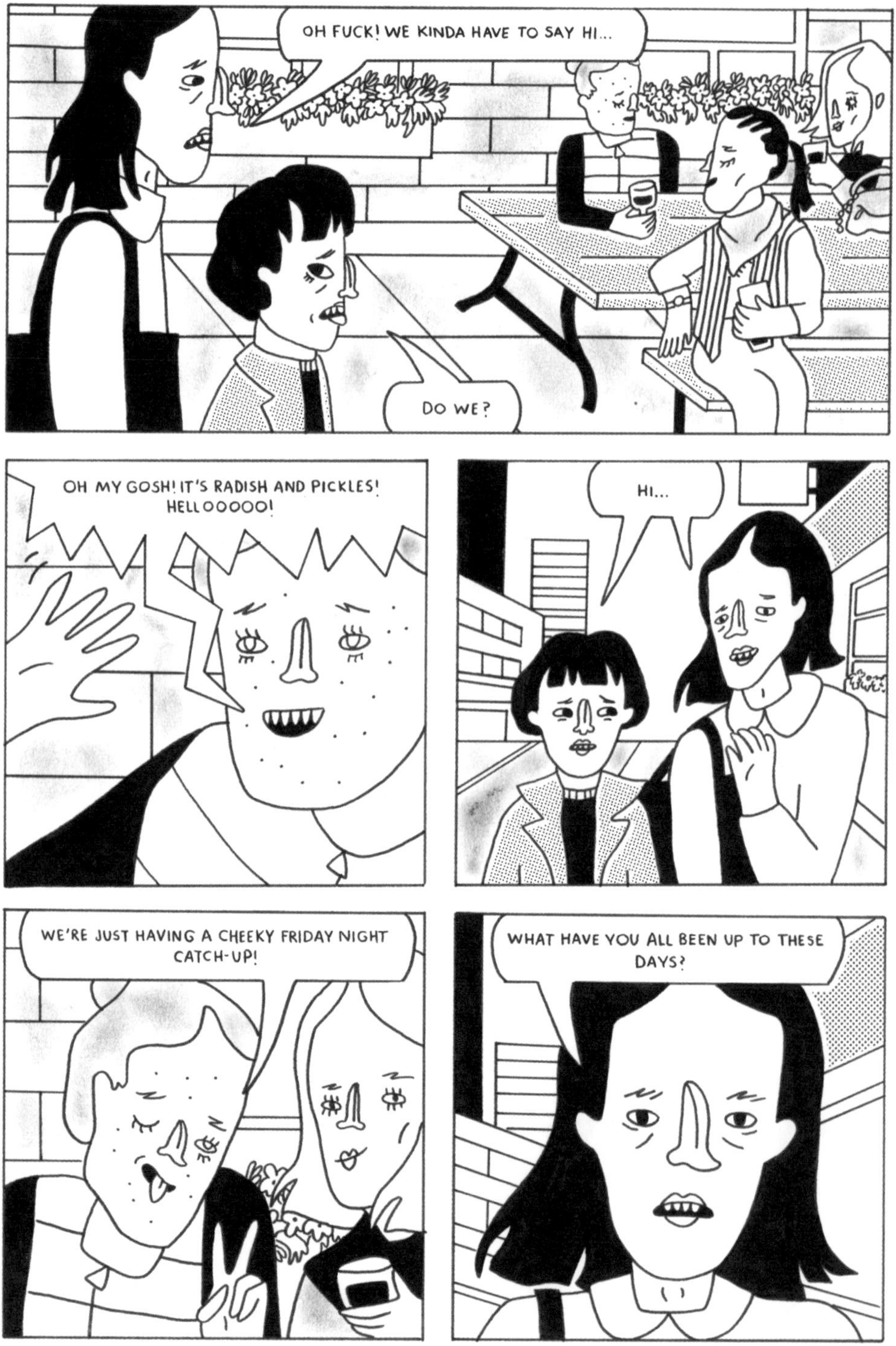
OH FUCK! WE KINDA HAVE TO SAY HI...
DO WE?
OH MY GOSH! IT'S RADISH AND PICKLES! HELLOOOOO!
HI...
WE'RE JUST HAVING A CHEEKY FRIDAY NIGHT CATCH-UP!
WHAT HAVE YOU ALL BEEN UP TO THESE DAYS?

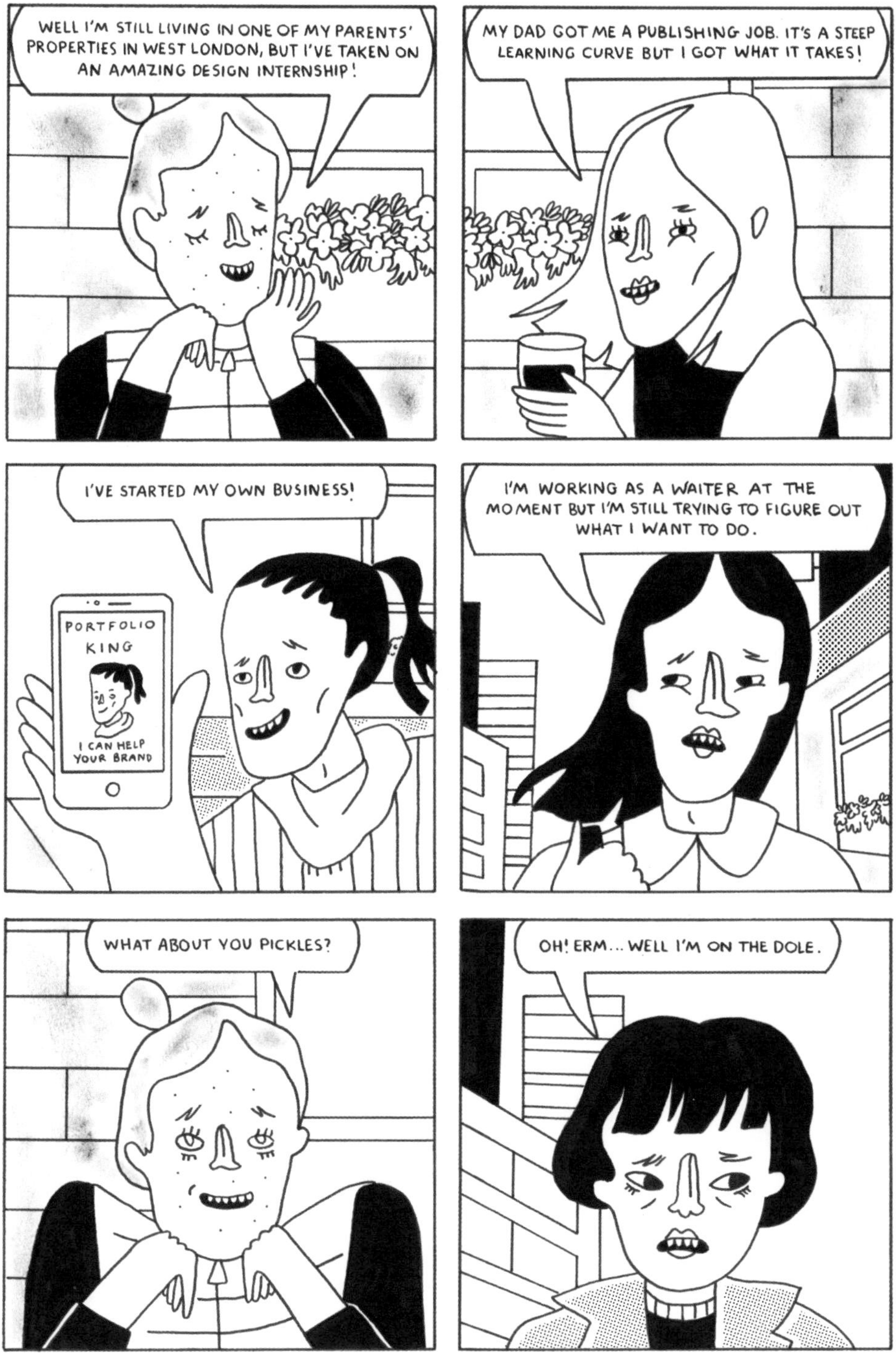
WELL I'M STILL LIVING IN ONE OF MY PARENTS' PROPERTIES IN WEST LONDON, BUT I'VE TAKEN ON AN AMAZING DESIGN INTERNSHIP!
MY DAD GOT ME A PUBLISHING JOB. IT'S A STEEP LEARNING CURVE BUT I GOT WHAT IT TAKES!
I'VE STARTED MY OWN BUSINESS!
PORTFOLIO KING
I CAN HELP YOUR BRAND
I'M WORKING AS A WAITER AT THE MOMENT BUT I'M STILL TRYING TO FIGURE OUT WHAT I WANT TO DO.
WHAT ABOUT YOU PICKLES?
OH! ERM... WELL I'M ON THE DOLE.

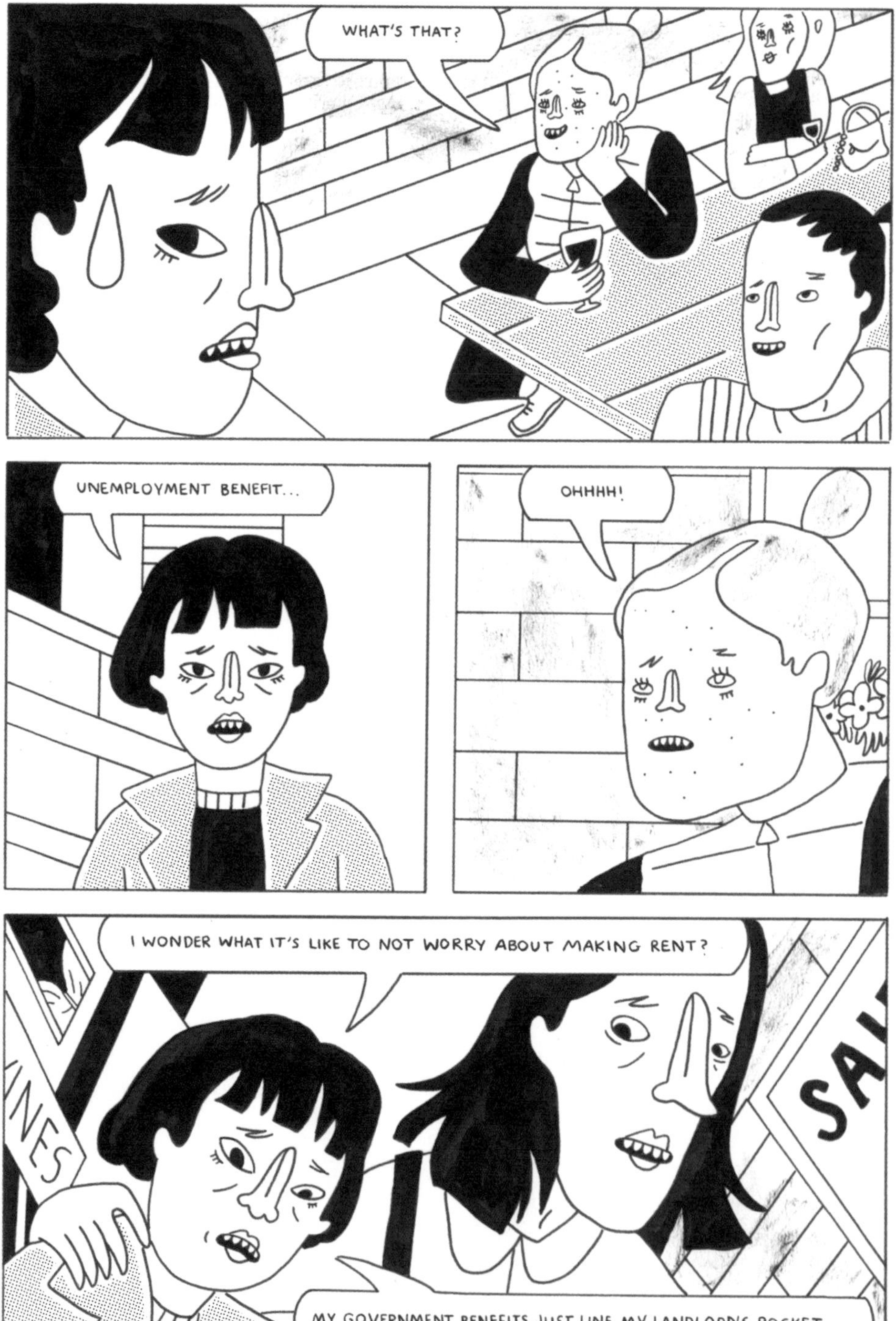
WHAT'S THAT?
UNEMPLOYMENT BENEFIT...
OHHHH!
I WONDER WHAT IT'S LIKE TO NOT WORRY ABOUT MAKING RENT?
MY GOVERNMENT BENEFITS JUST LINE MY LANDLORD'S POCKET...

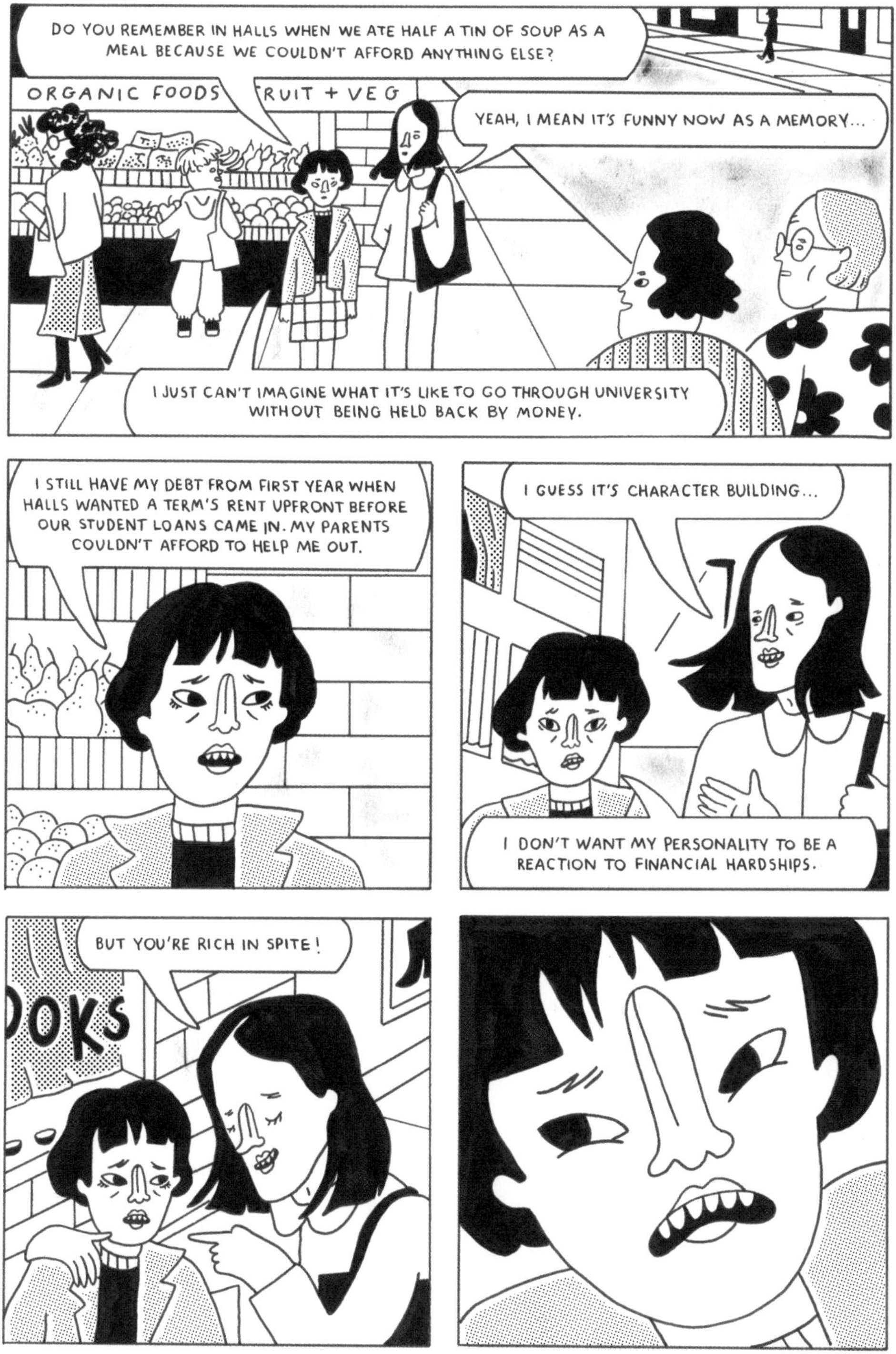
DO YOU REMEMBER IN HALLS WHEN WE ATE HALF A TIN OF SOUP AS A MEAL BECAUSE WE COULDN'T AFFORD ANYTHING ELSE?
ORGANIC FOODS
RUIT + VEG
YEAH, I MEAN IT'S FUNNY NOW AS A MEMORY...
I JUST CAN'T IMAGINE WHAT IT'S LIKE TO GO THROUGH UNIVERSITY WITHOUT BEING HELD BACK BY MONEY.
I STILL HAVE MY DEBT FROM FIRST YEAR WHEN HALLS WANTED A TERM'S RENT UPFRONT BEFORE OUR STUDENT LOANS CAME IN. MY PARENTS COULDN'T AFFORD TO HELP ME OUT.
I GUESS IT'S CHARACTER BUILDING...
I DON'T WANT MY PERSONALITY TO BE A REACTION TO FINANCIAL HARDSHIPS.
BUT YOU'RE RICH IN SPITE!
OOKS

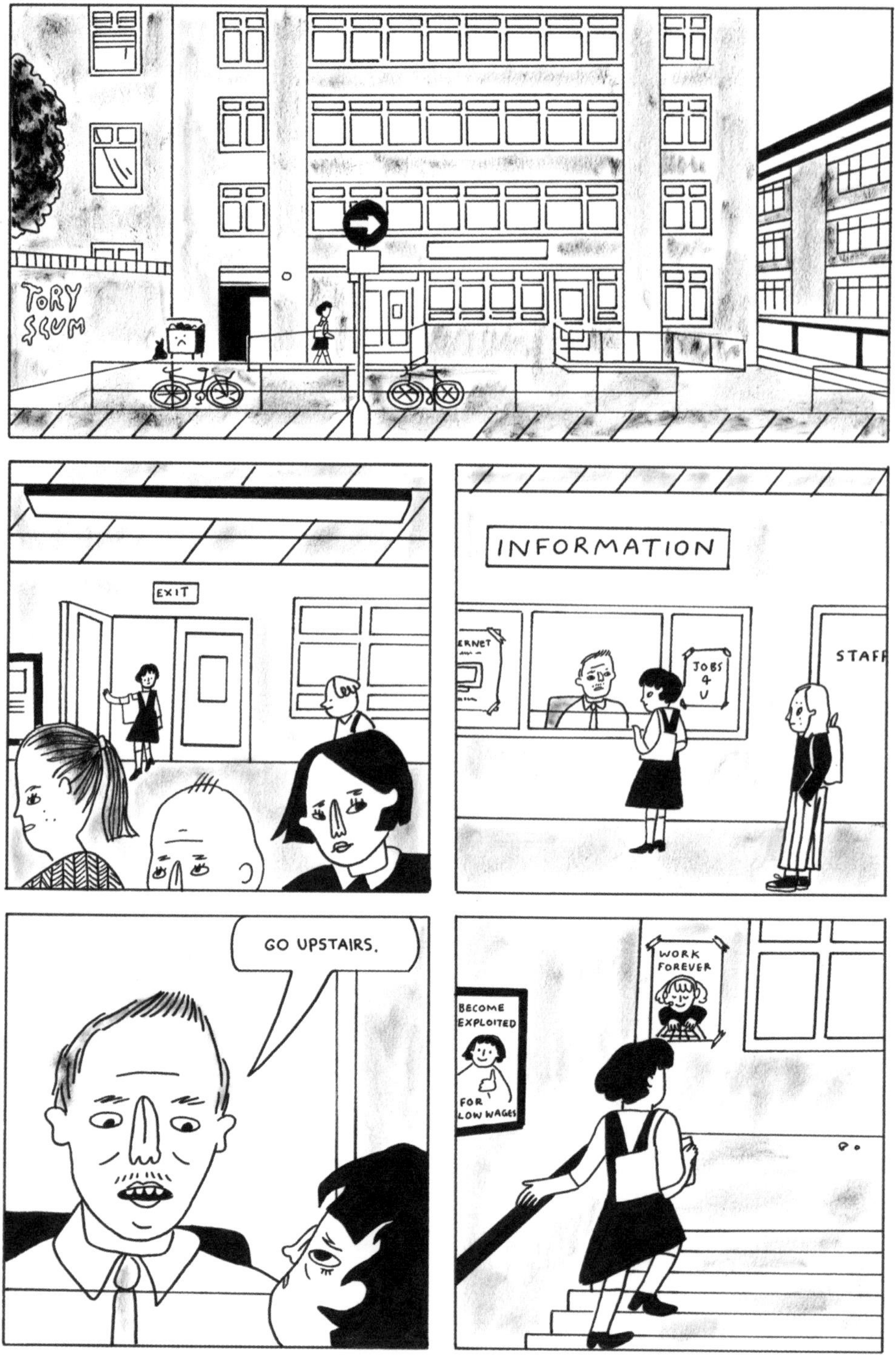
TORY SCUM
EXIT
INFORMATION
JOBS 4 U
GO UPSTAIRS.
WORK FOREVER
BECOME EXPLOITED
FOR LOW WAGES

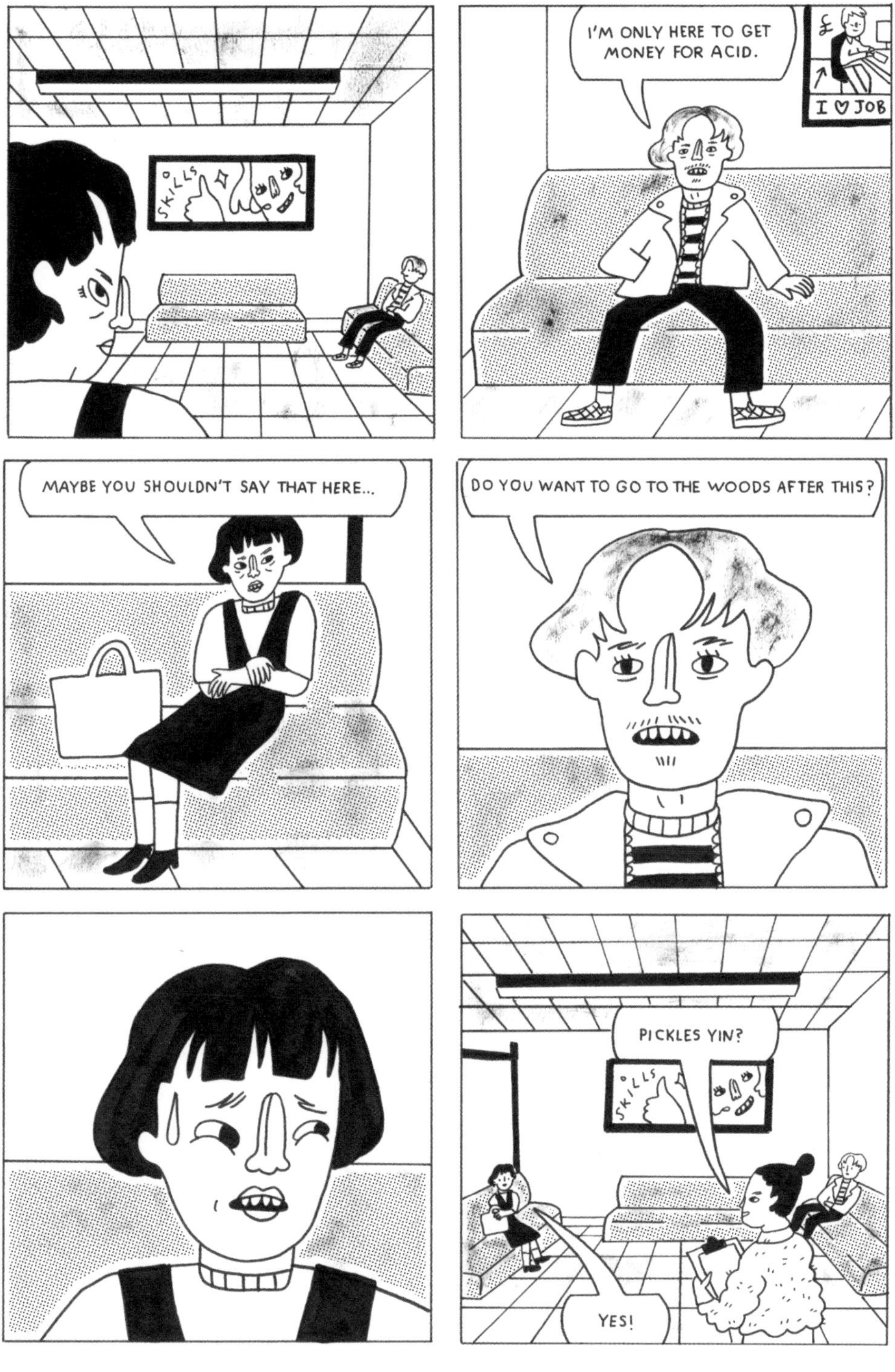
SKILLS
I'M ONLY HERE TO GET MONEY FOR ACID.
£
I ♡ JOB
MAYBE YOU SHOULDN'T SAY THAT HERE...
DO YOU WANT TO GO TO THE WOODS AFTER THIS?
PICKLES YIN?
SKILLS
YES!

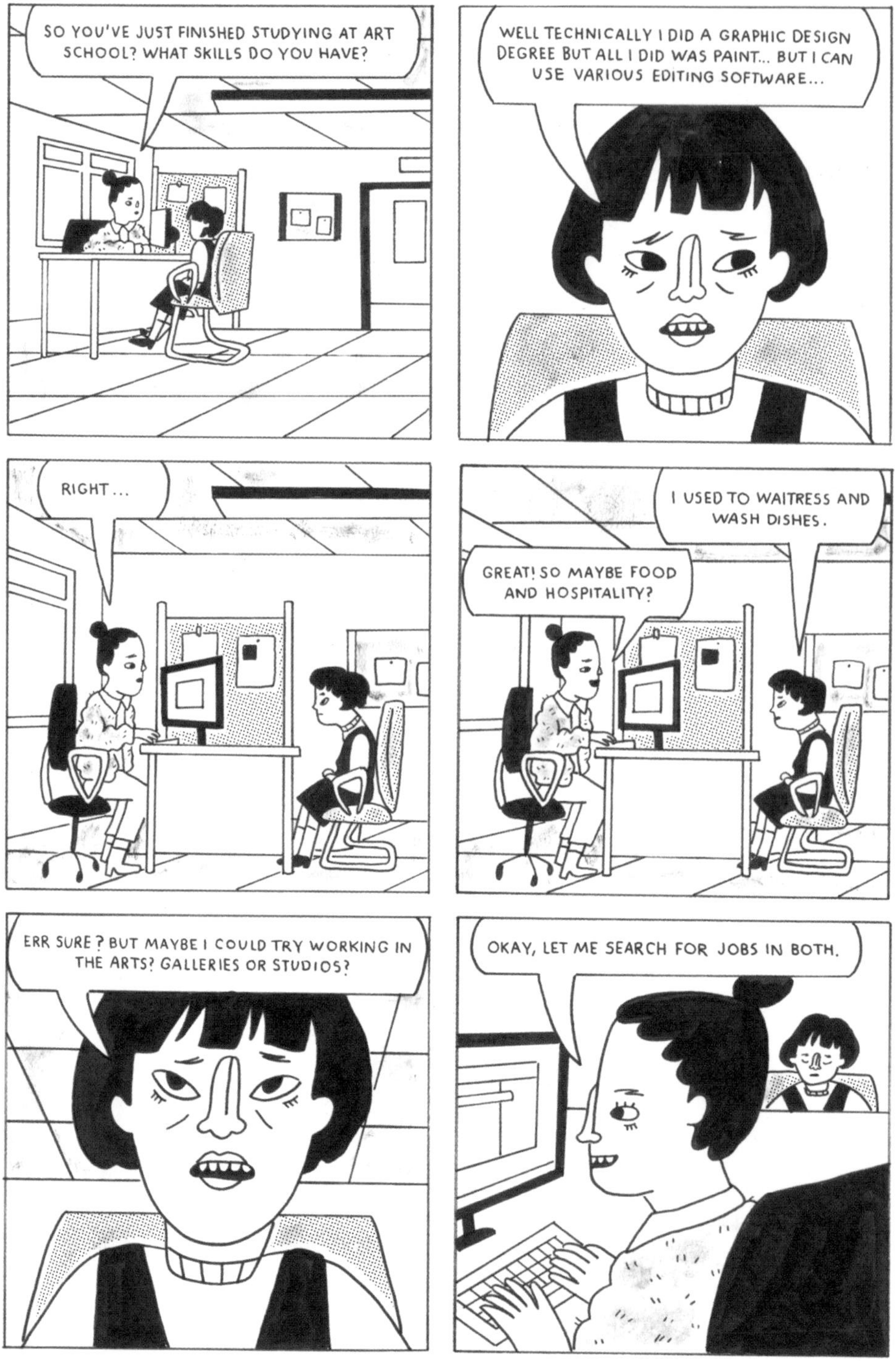
SO YOU'VE JUST FINISHED STUDYING AT ART SCHOOL? WHAT SKILLS DO YOU HAVE?
WELL TECHNICALLY I DID A GRAPHIC DESIGN DEGREE BUT ALL I DID WAS PAINT... BUT I CAN USE VARIOUS EDITING SOFTWARE...
RIGHT...
I USED TO WAITRESS AND WASH DISHES.
GREAT! SO MAYBE FOOD AND HOSPITALITY?
ERR SURE? BUT MAYBE I COULD TRY WORKING IN THE ARTS? GALLERIES OR STUDIOS?
OKAY, LET ME SEARCH FOR JOBS IN BOTH.

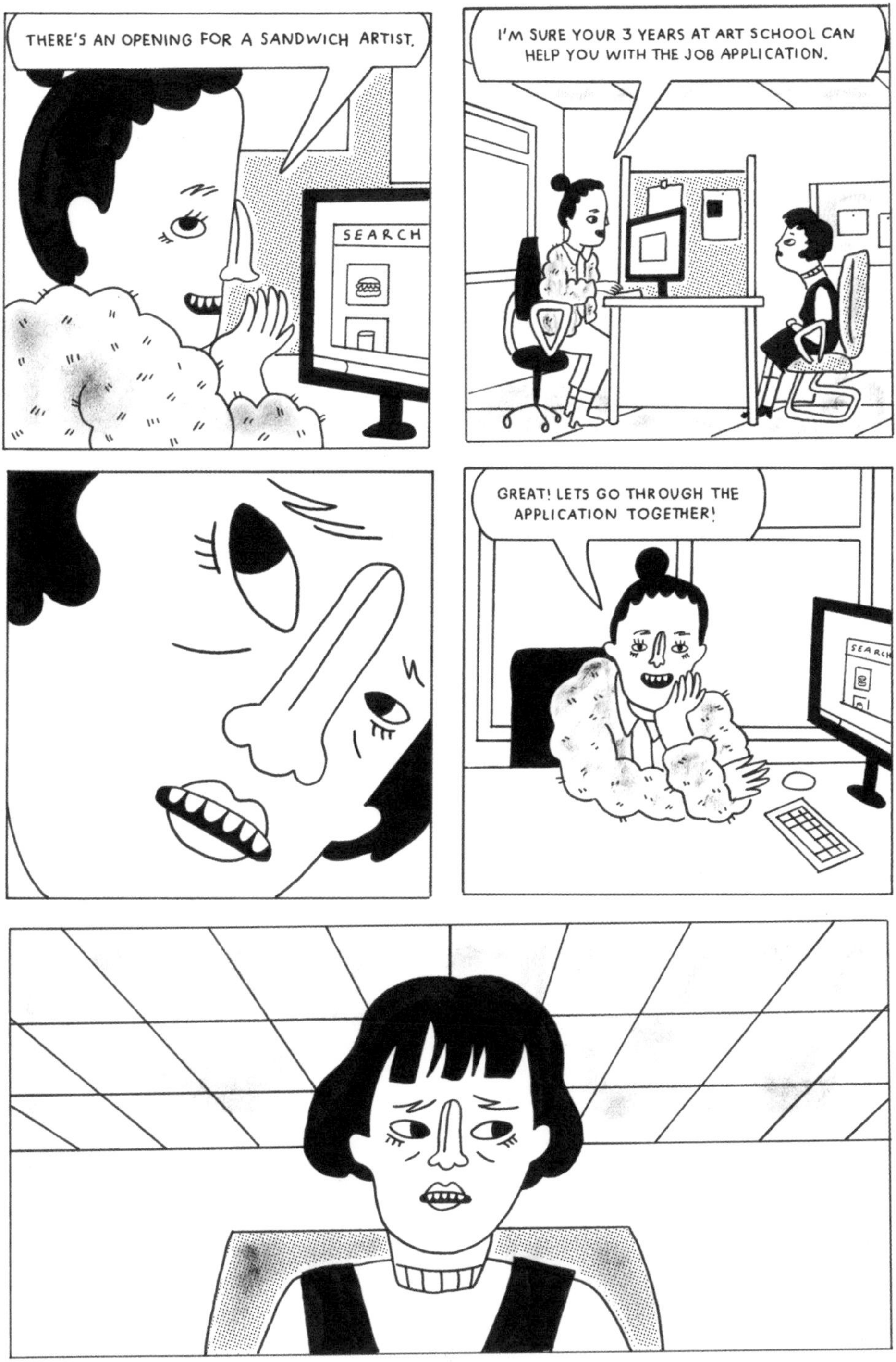
THERE'S AN OPENING FOR A SANDWICH ARTIST.
SEARCH
I'M SURE YOUR 3 YEARS AT ART SCHOOL CAN HELP YOU WITH THE JOB APPLICATION.
GREAT! LETS GO THROUGH THE APPLICATION TOGETHER!

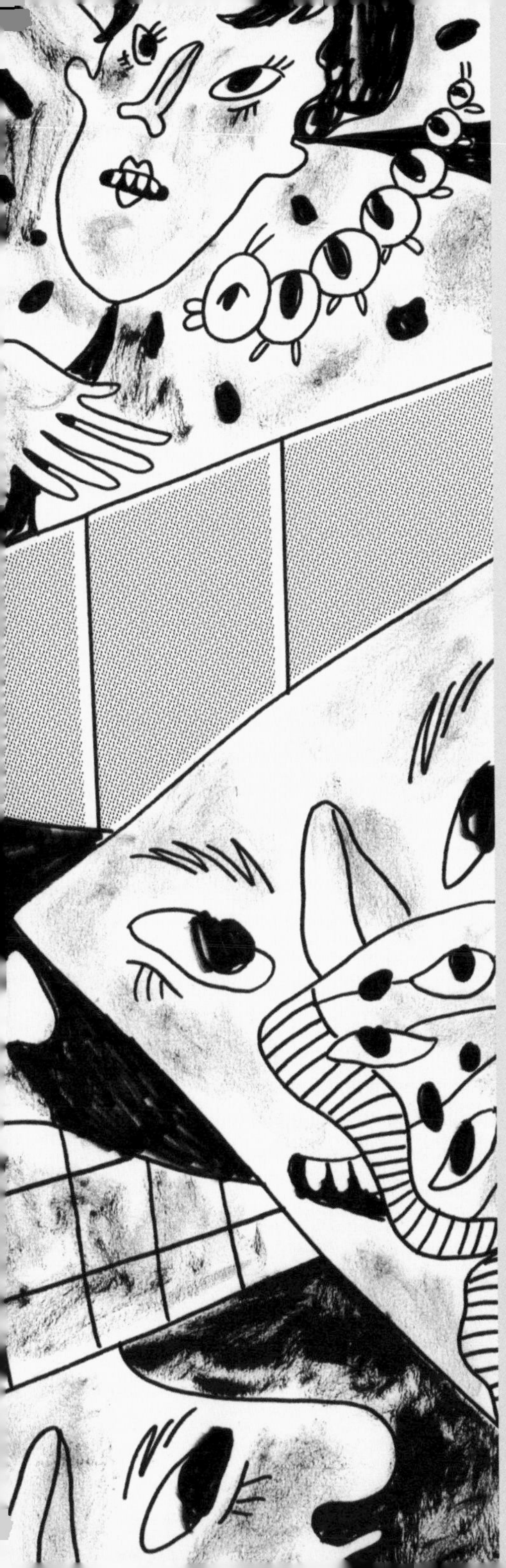

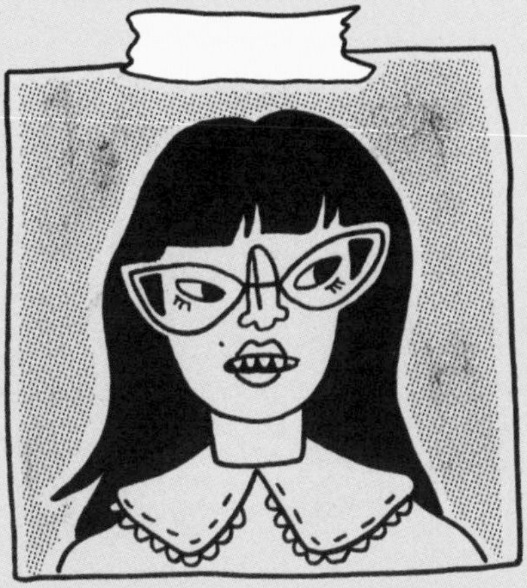

CLIO ISADORA WAS BORN IN 1991 IN MANCHESTER. SHE CURRENTLY LIVES IN LONDON WITH HER COLLECTION OF POKEMON PLUSHES AND CAT.

THANK YOU: THE AVERY HILL TEAM, METAL SOUTHEND / INKHEAD RESIDENCY, ROSE, JOJI, KAZU, POOH, THE WORMS, DRIBBLE, ALL MY ONLINE AND REAL LIFE FRIENDS (ESPECIALLY THE ONES THAT LISTENED TO ME WHINGE AND HELPED ME AT COMIC FAIRS OVER THE YEARS).

Cranston Public Library

3 1450 00869 6288

PUBLISHED BY AVERY HILL PUBLISHING, 2021

10 9 8 7 6 5 4 3 2 1

COPYRIGHT © CLIO ISADORA, 2021

CLIO ISADORA HAS ASSERTED THEIR RIGHT UNDER THE COPYRIGHT, DESIGNS
AND PATENTS ACT 1988 TO BE IDENTIFIED AS THE AUTHOR OF THIS WORK

ALL RIGHTS RESERVED. NO PORTION OF THIS BOOK MAY BE REPRODUCED,
STORED IN A RETRIEVAL SYSTEM, OR TRANSMITTED IN ANY FORM OR BY
ANY MEANS, MECHANICAL, ELECTRONIC, PHOTOCOPYING, RECORDING,
OR OTHERWISE, WITHOUT PRIOR WRITTEN PERMISSION FROM THE PUBLISHER

FIRST PUBLISHED IN THE UK IN 2021 BY
AVERY HILL PUBLISHING
UNIT 8
5 DURHAM YARD
LONDON

CRANSTON PUBLIC LIBRARY
CENTRAL

A CIP RECORD FOR THIS BOOK IS AVAILABLE FROM THE BRITISH LIBRARY

ISBN: 978-1-910395-63-9

CLIO ISADORA
WWW.CLIOISADORA.COM

AVERY HILL PUBLISHING
WWW.AVERYHILLPUBLISHING.COM

JAN - 3 2022